arctic
knits

TO MY MOM;
WHO DESIGNED HER OWN GARMENTS,
WHO I TAGGED ALONG WITH TO SEAMSTRESSES,
WHO I WISH COULD READ THIS.

arctic knits

jumpers, socks, hats and mittens

WEICHIEN CHAN

Photography by Kim Lightbody

Hardie Grant

QUADRILLE

CONTENTS

INTRODUCTION

Hello! I am weichien and I am the author of this little book. I am more commonly known as thepetiteknitter in the digital world of knitting.

I live on a remote island in the Canadian Arctic archipelago called Iqaluit. In my little corner of the world where winter lingers for more than half the year, I find comfort in making my own woolly garments.

In the depths of winter, I get up before the sun rises and get home after the sun sets. After wrestling my woollen hat, sealskin mitts, heavy duty boots and the extra three pounds of clothing I have on, I stumble through my door, greet saskie, my bunny, and start a fire in my wood stove. This ritual is a sure sign that the bitter and dark Arctic winter is upon us. I hear the wood pellets crackle in the fireplace. My home slowly warms up. My brain tells me it's time for knitting. I bundle up in a cozy corner, yarn laced around my fingers and get to work.

Many of you might not know, I was born in the tropics and moved to Canada in my late teens. I learned to knit from a dear friend, Alex, who I met while on a study exchange in Norway. Knitting culture is very much alive in the Nordics. Every dinner party brings at least one guest with a knitting project. Even though I never picked up knitting when living in Scandinavia, my time there has gently nudged me towards it.

I remember Christmas that year. I finished up my second exchange in Belgium. We were in Alex's old stomping ground, Nice. It was a balmy 20°C winter day on the Mediterranean coast. As we sat on the beach, I decided on a whim to learn to knit. Alex was beyond happy to oblige. Off we went on a yarn hunting mission. We settled on French merino wool.

The first thing I ever knitted was a colourblock garter stitch scarf. I stayed up way too late convincing myself I could master it by dawn. It was as if knitting was the full circle I needed to wrap up my time in Europe. A few days after picking up knitting needles for the first time in my life, I boarded my flight and returned to Canada. Three years later, I started thepetiteknitter and haven't looked back since. My first project barely resembled a scarf, but it took me on a journey I would have never imagined possible.

Knitting is slow, arguably the slowest of slow fashion. Every stitch in the art of knitting is intentional – from designing, swatching to actual knitting, every step in the process is a conscious choice. When you live on an Arctic island where no one is ever in a rush, you take for granted the thing everyone else in the rest of the universe wishes for more of – time.

ARCTIC KNITS is my first book and I am so excited, yet nervous, to share it with you all. I hope to take you on a virtual adventure through the Arctic tundra, a place that inspires me endlessly. A place I am so blessed to call home. I also hope that, through this book, we slow down, enjoy the little things around us and appreciate what we have. Thank you for joining me on my knitting journey. My heart is beyond full.

HOW TO USE THIS BOOK

ARCTIC KNITS is an exclusive collection of my knitting creations. You will find six jumpers and three mittens, hats and socks in this compact little book. Each garment is carefully designed for a timeless and classic look. It is thoughtfully curated for colourwork aficionados and made for knitters who enjoy creating cherished, loved and lasting heirloom pieces.

Whether you are a new or experienced colourwork knitter, you are sure to embark on a fun experience. This is a book where you can express your most colourful self and experiment with colours and contrasts. And if you are more of a neutrals person like me, you will enjoy all the earthy tones used in this book.

Fair Isle colourwork knitting is fairly straightforward because you're only ever dealing with knit stitches and, on the odd occasion, pesky floats. Even though it seems simple, I love the possibilities it offers. The patterns and motifs that can be created from this traditional Scottish technique are truly limitless. I also love how the various colour combinations present themselves so differently when knitted in Fair Isle. I think colourwork knitters can quite possibly be considered the painters of the knitting world.

Rather than a strict manual, I see my patterns as a guide. Each body is truly unique. I encourage modifications in any form to make the garment fit you best. The beauty of knitting is that you can add personal touches and make the pieces truly yours. Here are some helpful notes before you begin.

SIZING
My jumpers are size-inclusive and come in ten different teen and adult sizes. The range of sizes for the jumpers covers chest circumferences of 71–160cm (28–63in). Socks come in eleven sizes to fit toddlers up to adults. Hats and mittens come in three sizes.

FIT
I love a boxy and gender-neutral fit for all my jumpers, which come with two sleeve and body length options. You can choose to add shaping to customize your jumpers to the desired fit. Socks, hats and mittens come with a 10% negative ease to keep your feet, head and hands warm and snuggly.

CHARTS
Colourwork charts are read from right to left and bottom to top. All stitches in colourwork charts are knit stitches unless stated otherwise.

MEASUREMENTS
All listed measurements in this book are for finished garment or piece measurements and include the intended positive and negative ease for the project.

GAUGE
It is extremely important to take the time to make a swatch before starting any project, especially garments. Swatch with the colourwork section of the pattern in the round to achieve the most accurate gauge. This will help you pick the garment size that fits you best. Adjust needle size as needed. Block your swatch to get the most accurate gauge.

SCHEMATIC
Here is a quick guide on how to use the jumper schematics in this book.

A: CHEST – lift your arms and measure the widest section of your chest.

B1: SIDE LENGTH (CROPPED) – starting at your underarm, measure to the top of your natural waistline.

B2: SIDE LENGTH (REGULAR) – starting at your underarm, measure to the top of your hip bone.

C1: SLEEVE LENGTH (BRACELET) – with your arm slightly bent, measure from underarm to 5cm (2in) above your wrist.

C2: SLEEVE LENGTH (FULL) – with your arm slightly bent, measure from underarm to your wrist.

D: UPPER ARM – measure the widest section of your bicep.

E: WRIST CIRCUMFERENCE – measure around your wrist bone.

F: YOKE DEPTH – from your collarbone, measure down to below your chest.

The magic of handknitting is the ability to alter your knits to fit your body best. It is a way of creating garments that are unique and special to you and only you.

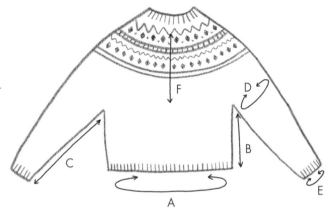

"ARCTIC WINTERS ARE LONG AND BITTER, WHILE THE SUMMERS ARE SHORT AND INTENSE. THE SUN SETS AT NOON IN THE PEAK OF WINTER AND IN THE DARKEST OF DAYS, I FIND SOLACE IN KNITTING."

KNITTING IN THE ARCTIC

ARCTIC KNITS is an ode to my life in the Arctic.

At a latitude of 60 degrees North, my home sits right below the Arctic Circle. Iqaluit, pronounced ee-cal-oo-it, means place of many fish in Inuktitut. In this arctic capital of the largest territory in Canada, we are located by the Arctic Ocean and are blessed with a polar climate. Contrary to popular belief, we experience four very distinct seasons. Our winters are long and dark, our springs refreshing and snowy, our summers intense and abundant, while our autumns are moody and cozy.

It typically starts snowing around late September and the Arctic Ocean freezes by the new year. In the peak of winter, dawn is at nine and dusk is at noon. Even though the sun hovers above the horizon on the shortest days, I am so thankful to catch a glimpse of it every day. I tend to struggle with the lack of daylight in winter and knitting helps distract me from it. But what I truly look forward to is chasing auroras that dance in the dark and frigid Arctic skies.

While 'April showers bring May flowers' rings true in most of the Northern hemisphere, the Arctic equivalent would be 'May blizzards bring June thaws'. The several feet of snow accumulation throughout the winter months requires fresh spring snow to hasten the thawing of the tundra.

If I had a favourite season, it would be Arctic spring. The light slowly returns and the soft, gentle snow days remind me of why I choose to live in the Arctic. It's the perfect season to travel across the frozen tundra and Arctic Ocean. Snowmobile rides are fun and if I am

feeling adventurous, I go on a dog sledding tour across the frozen bay. When luck is on my side, I sometimes chance upon Arctic hares hopping around the tundra.

Iqaluit is accessible only by plane. The closest metropolitan area to us is a three-and-a-half-hour flight away. Our groceries, necessities and mail are imported to us by cargo jets. Three times a year, we get sealifts by boat when the Arctic Ocean thaws for a few months. Most of us get furniture, building materials, vehicles and large appliances on these sealifts. The excitement when sealift season is around the corner is something that only a northerner will fathom. As I am writing this, the first boat of the season is due to arrive in a month's time. I can almost feel the buzz around it. This year is special as we have a brand new port!

Living this far north teaches me a lot about patience. If you missed this year's sealift, you will have to wait at least a year to get your items. The things most people take for granted – walking into the store and getting exactly what you are looking for – is a luxury we do not enjoy. There are days where the produce shelves in our two grocery stores are empty because the plane cannot land. There are times when our main water supply is contaminated and we run out of fresh drinking water and have to fly water in from the south. There is no such thing as shopping at a local yarn store. As a knitter who lives in the north, choosing colours online is by far the most challenging thing for me! My yarn crosses oceans and lands to get to me and I treasure every little skein I have.

Not having access to malls and stores has also taught me to want less, to need less. It has taught me to embrace minimalism. The less I have, the less I truly need. With no fast fashion stores in sight, no opportunities for window shopping or impulse buying, every purchase I make becomes intentional. It makes me appreciate the things I have. It teaches me to value the art of hand making.

Most people think the tundra is barren, snowy, and white. However, it comes alive in summer. The tundra feeds us with Arctic fireweed for jam, blueberries for pies, cottongrass for our vases, while the Arctic waters bring us Arctic char and the freshest potable water. In the long summer days where the sun doesn't set, I spend my time collecting cottongrass, drying them and hanging bouquets in the little corners of my home. We forage berries and mushrooms and little keepsakes. Summer knitting is a little slower, gentler, and kinder. The days are long and the light is abundant.

The tundra is home to a habitat of animals that thrive in the polar climate. It is a playground for polar bears, muskoxen, Arctic foxes, Arctic hares, belugas, narwhals, caribou and walruses. Iqaluit truly lives up to its name as the place of many fish. We enjoy an abundance of Arctic char every year – in true tundra-to-table fashion. I love having fresh and raw Arctic char on a bed of steamed rice.

I like to say that it is sweater weather all year long in the Arctic. While there is a lot of truth to that, I have come to realize that it is an excuse I have created for myself to justify my knitting. There is something so satisfying about making your own garments one stitch at a time.

It is slow, intentional, and purposeful. In our world where everything is focused on efficiency, it feels good to produce something with my own hands. It teaches me to appreciate the beauty of slowing down and hand making.

The tundra is my palette. My knitwear is a translation of my life north of 60 degrees. It encompasses my experiences, my views, my landscapes, and my love for the Arctic I am so lucky to call home. While knitting my designs, I hope you enjoy a little piece of the Arctic tundra through my eyes.

TOOLS AND TECHNIQUES

TOOLS

CIRCULAR NEEDLES
To knit in the round for jumpers and hats.

SHORT CIRCULAR NEEDLES
To knit in the round for socks and mittens.

DOUBLE POINTED NEEDLES
To knit in the round for the crown of hats, sleeves, sock heels and toes, and thumb on mittens.

TAPESTRY NEEDLE
For weaving ends in and securing stitches.

STITCH MARKERS
Used to mark the beginning of the round or a section of stitches to return to.

SCRAP YARN OR STITCH HOLDER
Used to hold and secure stitches that are not being worked.

MEASURING TAPE
For measuring the body and garment for sizing.

SCISSORS
To cut off the working yarn or yarn ends.

BLOCKING BOARD
For placing garments to block after soaking and washing.

BLOCKING PINS
Used to secure and hold your garment shape in place when blocking.

TOWEL
To absorb excess water from your knits after soaking and washing for blocking.

GAUGE RULER
Used to measure swatches and verify needle sizes.

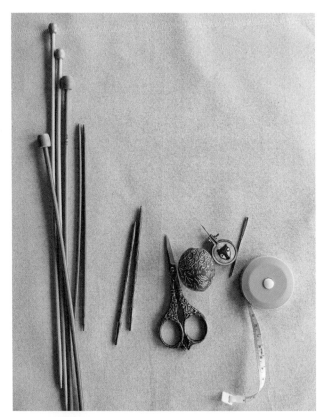

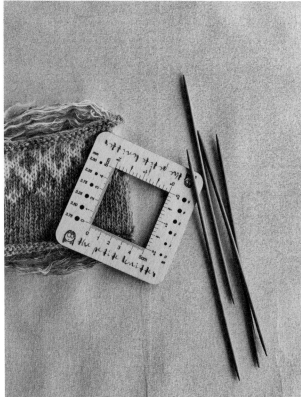

YARNS

There are many types of yarn in the fiber arts world, but they are composed of two main materials – natural fibers and synthetic fibers.

Natural fibers are yarn we can harvest from the earth. They come from both animals and plants. Animals like sheep, alpaca, goat, angora rabbit, muskoxen, silk worms and camels produce a wide variety of yarn – wool, mohair, cashmere, qiviut and silk. Amongst the most popular fibers that plants give us are cotton, hemp, flax and bamboo.Synthetic fibers are human-made fibers through chemical synthesis. Examples of synthetic fibers are polyester, acrylic, nylon and rayon.

I am drawn to natural fibers that are sustainable and ethically produced in a way where it does not harm the animals. I also prefer undyed or botanically dyed natural fibers.

As a knitter living in the far north, sheep's wool is by far my favourite fiber to work with. It is warm, durable, adaptable and water repellent. It traps air to keep me warm in the depths of winter and handles wear and tear well with all the shovelling I have to do. Undyed wool comes in the most gorgeous shades of brown, beige and grey, which reminds me of the tundra.

Cashmere is also a top choice for my designs. Who doesn't love a little luxury? Cashmere is warm, extremely soft and luxurious. It is always a treat to work with cashmere.

I have also recently developed a love for unspun yarn. It is rustic, usually undyed and comes in the shape of what knitters call plates. While it tends to break easily if tugged hard, it creates the airy-est and lightest fabric when knitted up. With enough practice and patience, unspun yarn will rarely break. It also works very well with mohair to create a fuzzy and cozy garment.

I am mindful of where I get my yarn and only choose to work with yarn providers that ethically source their wool, respect the environment and the animals, and embrace sustainable practices.

YARN SUBSTITUTES

Knitters often have preferred yarn they love to work with. The yarn in this book is a mini collection of the fibers I personally enjoy knitting with. You can substitute with any yarns you prefer. Try to stick to the same yarn weight and remember to swatch to ensure your gauge matches.

ABBREVIATIONS

This is a list of abbreviations used in this book and commonly used in knitting lexicons. You can refer to it as you work through the patterns.

bor – beginning of rnd

cc – contrasting colour

co – cast on

cont – continue

dec – decrease(s)

in – inches

inc – increase(s)

k – knit

k2tog – knit two stitches together

m1 – make one stitch

mc – main colour

p – purl

pm – place marker

rem – remaining

rep – repeat

rnd(s) – round(s)

rs – right side

sr – short row

sl – slip

ssk – slip slip knit

st(s) – stitch(es)

w&t – wrap and turn

ws – wrong side

** – repeat instruction between asterisks

BACKWARDS LOOP CAST-ON

The backwards loop cast-on is used to create extra stitches for the underarm hole in jumpers.

TOOLS: Working yarn, knitting needle

STEP 1: Have the right side of your work facing you. Hold your working yarn on your left hand to prepare for a slip knot loop.

STEP 2: Using the working yarn, make a loop. Ensure the yarn connected to the needle is at the bottom.

STEP 3: Slip your needle through the loop from the front.

STEP 4: Tug on the working yarn to tighten the stitch. You have cast on one stitch.

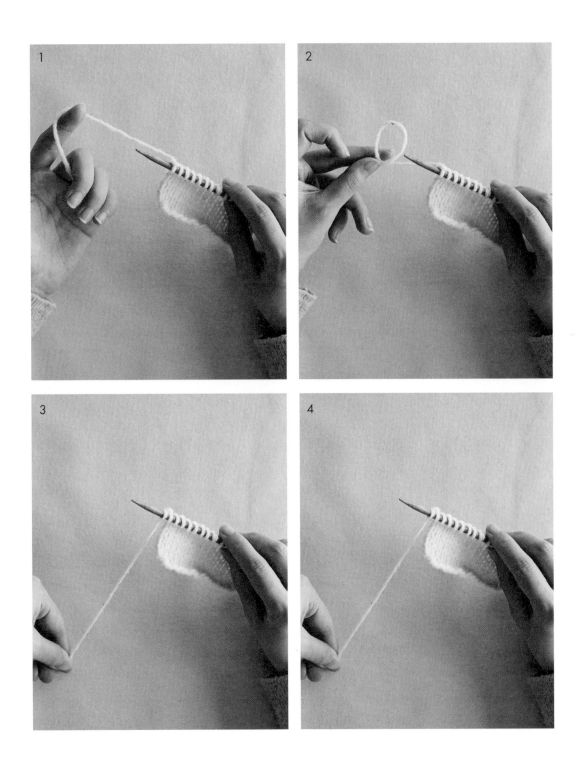

KITCHENER STITCH

Kitchener stitch is used to graft live stitches together. It is used for toes and heels in socks.

TOOLS: Working yarn, two knitting needles, tapestry needle

SET UP: Divide the stitches evenly across two needles. Ensure wrong sides face each other. Thread the working yarn through a tapestry needle.

STEP 1: Insert the tapestry needle through the first stitch on the front needle purl wise. Pull yarn through, leaving the stitch on the needle.

STEP 2: Insert tapestry needle through the first stitch on the back needle knit wise. Pull the yarn through, leaving the stitch on the needle.

STEP 3: Insert the tapestry needle through the first stitch on the front needle knit wise.

STEP 4: Pull the yarn through, slip that stitch off the needle.

STEP 5: Insert the tapestry needle through the next stitch on the front needle purl wise. Pull the yarn through, leaving that stitch on the needle.

STEP 6: Insert the tapestry needle through the first stitch on the back needle purl wise.

STEP 7: Pull the yarn through, slip that stitch off the needle.

STEP 8: Insert the tapestry needle through the next stitch on the back needle knit wise. Pull the yarn through, leaving that stitch on the needle.

Rep Steps 3 to 6 until all stitches are grafted. Break the working yarn and move the tail inside the work. Weave in ends.

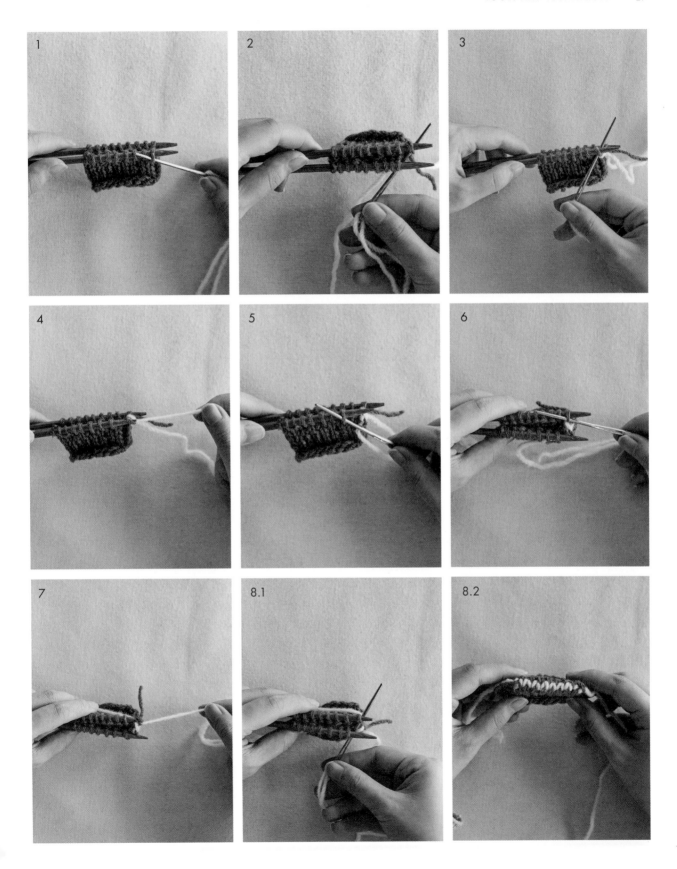

CATCHING LONG FLOATS

On the wrong side of colourwork knitting, there are floats (strands of yarn that extend from the last point on a row that a colour was used to the next point).

When the design has a long stretch of stitches in one colour, you should catch your floats. I usually catch floats when same-colour stitches are more than six stitches apart.

TOOLS: Working yarn, knitting needle

STEP 1: With the working yarn, work half the stitches required for the long stretch.

STEP 2: Bring the non-working yarn over the working yarn – the working yarn will trap it against the back of the work with the next stitch.

STEP 3: Work the next stitches as normal with the working yarn. You have caught the float!

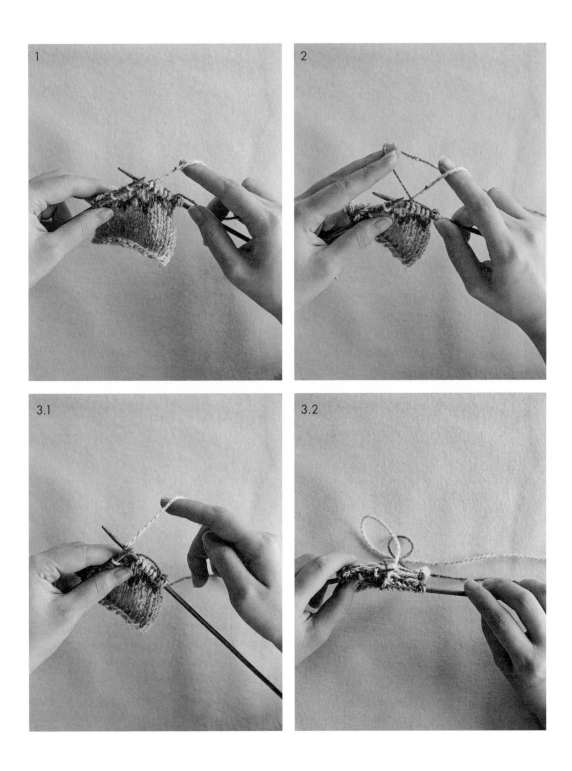

AFTERTHOUGHT HEEL

The afterthought heel is arguably the simplest heel technique in the knitting world. It works very well with colourwork socks.

TOOLS: Working yarn, knitting needle, scrap yarn, tapestry needle

STEP 1: Leaving a tail of scrap yarn hanging, knit across the heel stitches using the scrap yarn as required in the pattern.

STEP 2: Slip the scrap yarn stitches from your right hand needle back onto your left hand needle.

STEP 3: Knit the scrap yarn stitches using your working yarn. Continue knitting the pattern as indicated until the sock is complete.

STEP 4: Using a needle, pick up the number of stitches indicated in the pattern below the scrap yarn.

STEP 5: Using another needle, pick up the number of stitches as indicated in the pattern above the scrap yarn.

STEP 6: Remove scrap yarn. You are now ready to knit the heel.

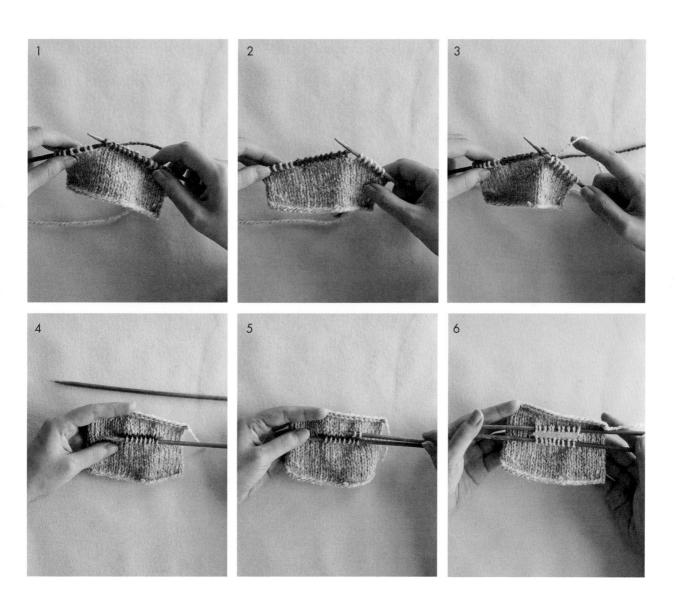

CORRUGATED RIBBING

Corrugated ribbing adds an elevated touch to regular ribbing. The trick to corrugated ribbing is in the set-up round. It is important to note that corrugated is less stretchy than regular ribbing. It is recommended to swatch and size up knitting needles if necessary. To demonstrate this technique, we will use 1x1 rib.

STEP 1: Using colour A, knit one stitch. Using colour B, knit the next stitch. Repeat this sequence to the end of the round.

STEP 2: Using colour A, knit one stitch. Ensure both working yarns are at the back.

STEP 3: Bring colour B working yarn to the front. Purl one stitch using colour B. Move colour B working yarn to the back. Repeat Step 2 and 3 to end of the round.

STEP 4: Repeat Steps 2 and 3 until your ribbing measures your desired length.

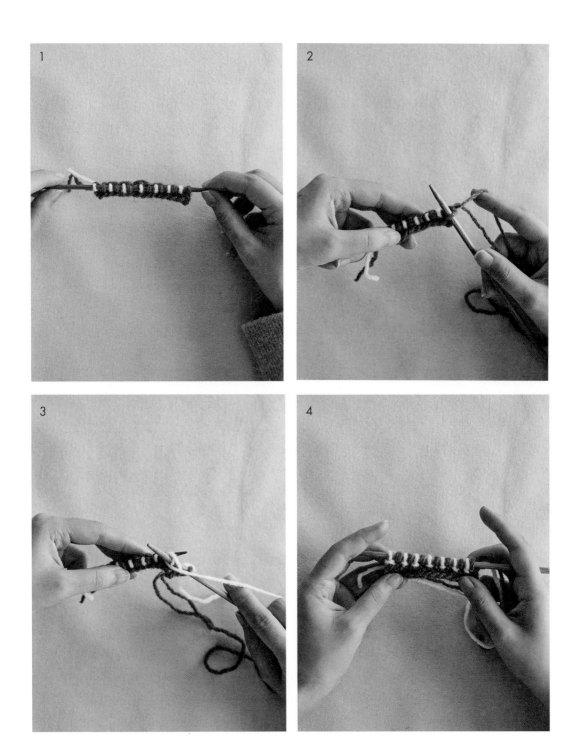

"IF I HAD A FAVOURITE SEASON,
IT WOULD BE ARCTIC SPRING.
THE LIGHT SLOWLY RETURNS AND
THE SOFT, GENTLE SNOW DAYS
REMIND ME OF WHY I CHOOSE
TO LIVE IN THE ARCTIC."

BLOCKING

Blocking is an essential step in the knitting process that is often overlooked. I don't consider my projects completed until I block them. Blocking sets the stitches, plumps up the fibers, and often softens the garments. It transforms hand knits from a work-in-progress to a beautiful wearable item. Fill up a sink or tub with lukewarm water and completely submerge your garment. Soak it for 15–30 minutes.

Remember to check your manufacturer's recommendations for soaking times and water temperature. You can add a small amount of delicate detergent or wool soap. Remember to rinse until the water is clear if you choose to use soap.

Remove your garment and gently squeeze to remove water. Do not wring. Lay it flat on a dry, absorbent towel, then roll up the garment in the towel. Press firmly on the roll to squeeze out excess water from the garment and into the towel. Then lay the garment flat on a blocking mat and carefully pull the item to the desired shape and intended measurements. Use blocking pins to secure the edges to the mat, then leave it air dry.

WASHING AND STORING

Here are a few tips to help your hand knits last longer.

WASHING

Wool rarely needs washing unless you soil or stain it. Certain types of wool like Istex Lopi are self-cleaning. The lanolin on the untreated wool is what makes it breathable and self-cleaning. Garments knitted out of these wools do not need washing. A good airing after each wear is adequate.

If you choose to wash your knits, use gentle detergent or wool soap. Fill a tub or sink with cold water and mix well with your soap of choice. Soak your knit and gently rub it in the water, ensuring you do not wring the garment. Rinse your knit till the water is clear. To remove the water from your knit, lay it flat on a dry absorbent towel. Roll up the garment in the towel. Press firmly on the roll to squeeze out excess water from the garment and into the towel. Again, do not wring the towel. Place your knit on a blocking board and shape the item to its original form. Use blocking pins if desired. Let it air dry.

STORAGE

We are blessed with no moths in the Arctic. I like to fold my knits in a stack and store them on a wooden shelf in my studio. However, in the rest of the world where moths exist, the best way to keep your knits is to store them in a cedar box in a cool and dry place. For additional protection against insects, store them in a resealable plastic bag. Do not hang your hand knits. This will stretch them out as the weight of the garments will strain the stitches. You run the risk of misshaping the hand knits from the shape of the hanger, too.

THE
PROJECTS

ARCTICA JUMPER

Arctica is a modern take on the ancient continent of Arctida. It is a collection of my tundra life. When the day comes when I have to leave the Arctic, I will have my Arctica to remind me of this chapter of my life.

NOTES

This jumper pattern is unisex, has a boxy fit, and comes in ten adult sizes. There are two options for body length – cropped and regular. Because the jumper is knitted top-down, you can easily customize the length by stopping before or continuing after the recommended body length measurements. There are also two sleeve length options – bracelet and full length – so you can customize the jumper to fit you best. As each body is unique, please remember that the pattern serves as a guide. Feel free to modify any lengths to fit your own body and arms. The colourwork chart is read from right to left, bottom to top. The intended ease is about 10cm/4in to 18cm/7in. Remember to swatch to check gauge and size up or down with needles as needed.

CONSTRUCTION

This jumper is knitted top-down and in the round. You begin at the neck, which is followed by a seamless colourwork round yoke that expands in width with regular increases. There is optional short-row shaping to raise the back of the neck and also to create more room about the chest area, to suit your preferences. Once the yoke is complete, you separate for the sleeves to create armholes and then continue with the body. When you have knitted the body you return to the held stitches you separated for each sleeve. The tapered sleeves are knitted top-down and in the round as well.

SIZES

1 (2, 3, 4) 5, 6 [7, 8, 9] 10

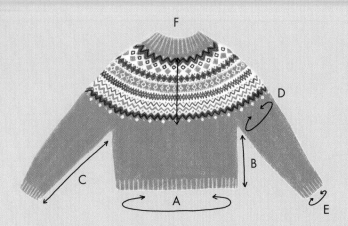

HOW TO PICK A SIZE

For a comfortable fit, this jumper should be worn with a recommended positive ease of 10cm/4in to 18cm/7in. Measure the widest section of your chest with a measuring tape. For example, your chest measurement is 102cm/40¼in. If you prefer less positive ease, you should pick size 3 for a positive ease of 5cm/2in. If you prefer more positive ease, you should pick size 4 for a positive ease of 18cm/7in.

MEASUREMENTS

A: CHEST CIRCUMFERENCE
cm: 91 (104, 113, 129) 140, 151 [164, 178, 189] 200
in: 36½ (42, 45¼, 51½) 56, 60½ [66, 71, 75½] 80

B1: SIDE LENGTH – CROPPED
cm: 20.5 (20.5, 20.5, 20.5) 20.5, 20.5 [20.5, 20.5, 20.5] 20.5
in: 8 (8, 8, 8) 8, 8 [8, 8, 8] 8

B2: SIDE LENGTH – REGULAR
cm: 33 (35.5, 38, 40.5) 43.5, 46 [47, 49, 49] 51
in: 13 (14, 15, 16) 17¼, 18¼ [18½, 19¼, 19¼] 20

C1: SLEEVE LENGTH – BRACELET
cm: 48.5 (49.5, 49.5, 51) 51, 52 [52, 53.5, 53.5] 53.5
in: 19¼ (19½, 19½, 20) 20, 20½ [20½, 21, 21] 21

C2: SLEEVE LENGTH – FULL
cm: 50.5 (51.5, 52, 53.5) 56, 57 [58.5, 58.5, 59.5] 60
in: 20 (20¼, 20½, 21) 22, 22½ [23, 23, 23½] 23¾

D: UPPER ARM
cm: 35.6 (35.6, 38.9, 42) 47.8, 50 [52, 58.9, 60] 61
in: 14 (14, 15¼, 16½) 18¾, 18¾ [20½, 23¼, 23½] 24

E: WRIST CIRCUMFERENCE
cm: 20.5 (21, 21, 21.5) 23, 23 [23, 23, 23] 24
in: 8 (8¼, 8¼, 8½) 9, 9 [9, 9, 9] 9½

F: YOKE DEPTH
cm: 25 (25, 25, 25.5) 25.5, 25.5 [25.5, 26.5, 26.5] 26.5
in: 9¾ (9¾, 9¾, 10) 10, 10 [10, 10½, 10½] 10½

YARN
Istex Léttlopi (100% pure new wool, aran (worsted) weight)

SAMPLE 1
mc – 0086 Light beige
cc1 – 0051 White
cc2 – 1419 Barley
cc3 – 0867 Chocolate

SAMPLE 2
mc – 0867 Chocolate
cc1 – 0051 White
cc2 – 1419 Barley
cc3 – 9427 Rust

SAMPLE 1

SAMPLE 2

YARDAGE
METRES – CROPPED
mc: 721 (805, 900, 1051) 1183, 1335 [1447, 1558, 1680] 1787
cc1: 100 (116, 124, 135) 143, 159 [163, 178, 186] 205
cc2: 100 (116, 124, 135) 143, 159 [163, 178, 186] 205
cc3: 80 (92, 98, 108) 114, 126 [130, 141, 148] 151

YARDS – CROPPED
mc: 788 (880, 984, 1149) 1294, 1460 [1582, 1704, 1837] 1954
cc1: 109 (127, 136, 148) 157, 174 [178, 195, 204] 224
cc2: 109 (127, 136, 148) 157, 174 [178, 195, 204] 224
cc3: 88 (101, 107, 118) 125, 138 [143, 155, 162] 165

METRES – REGULAR
mc: 860 (975, 1075, 1210) 1380, 1530 [1630, 1830, 1940] 2035
cc1: 100 (116, 124, 135) 143, 159 [163, 178, 186] 205
cc2: 100 (116, 124, 135) 143, 159 [163, 178, 186] 205
cc3: 80 (92, 98, 108) 114, 126 [130, 141, 148] 151

YARDS – REGULAR
mc: 941 (1067, 1176, 1324) 1510, 1673 [1782, 2001, 2120] 2225
cc1: 109 (127, 136, 148) 157, 174 [178, 195, 204] 224
cc2: 109 (127, 136, 148) 157, 174 [178, 195, 204] 224
cc3: 88 (101, 107, 118) 125, 138 [143, 155, 162] 165

GAUGE
18 sts x 24 rnds = 10cm/4in in colourwork sts and stockinette st

NEEDLES
Size 5mm/US8 or size necessary to obtain gauge. Use fixed circular knitting needles or cables for interchangeable needles in the following lengths:
40cm/16in
60cm/24in
80cm/32in

NOTIONS
Stitch markers
Tapestry needle
Scrap yarn

BEGIN PATTERN – NECK
Using 5mm/US8 needles and mc, co 84 (84, 84, 88) 96, 96 [100, 100, 100] 104 sts. Join in the rnd and pm to mark bor (at left back shoulder).
Work *k1, p1* ribbing until work measures 5cm/2in from co edge.

NECK SHAPING (OPTIONAL)
K 1 rnd.
Begin short-row shaping. Work in st st, picking up wraps as you come to them.
SR1 (rs): K 42 (42, 42, 44) 48, 48 [50, 50, 50] 52, w&t.
SR2 (ws): P 63 (63, 63, 66) 72, 72 [75, 75, 75] 78, w&t.
SR3 (rs): K 58 (58, 58, 61) 67, 67 [70, 70, 70] 73, w&t.
SR4 (ws): P 53 (53, 53, 56) 62, 62 [65, 65, 65] 68, w&t.
SR5 (rs): wK 48 (48, 48, 51) 57, 57 [60, 60, 60] 63, w&t.
SR6 (ws): P 43 (43, 43, 46) 52, 52 [55, 55, 55] 58, w&t.
SR7 (rs): K – (–, –, 41) 47, 47 [50, 50, 50] 53, w&t.
SR8 (ws): P – (–, –, 36) 42, 42 [45, 45, 45] 48, w&t.
With rs facing, k 1 round, picking up rem wraps and knitting them together with the wrapped sts as you go.

YOKE
Before working the chart, knit the following inc rounds to set up the yoke. Refer to the section correlating with your chosen size. As the width of the work expands while you work on the yoke, switch to longer circular needles (or cables, if you are using interchangeable needles) for your comfort.

SIZE 1
Rnd 1: K to end of rnd.
Rnd 2: *K14, m1* to end of rnd (6 inc). [90 sts]
Rnd 3: K to end of rnd.
Rnd 4: *K15, m1* to end of rnd (6 inc). [96 sts]

SIZE 2
Rnd 1: K to end of rnd.
Rnd 2: *K8, m1* to last 4 sts, k4 (10 inc). [94 sts]
Rnd 3: K to end of rnd.
Rnd 4: *K9, m1* to last 4 sts, k4 (10 inc). [104 sts]

SIZE 3
Rnd 1: K to end of rnd.
Rnd 2: *K6, m1* to end of rnd (14 inc). [98 sts]
Rnd 3: K to end of rnd.
Rnd 4: *K7, m1* to end of rnd (14 inc). [112 sts]

SIZE 4
Rnd 1: K to end of rnd.
Rnd 2: *K11, m1* to end of rnd (8 inc). [96 sts]
Rnd 3: K to end of rnd.
Rnd 4: *K6, m1* to end of rnd (16 inc). [112 sts]
Rnd 5: K to end of rnd.
Rnd 6: *K7, m1* to end of rnd (16 inc). [128 sts]

SIZE 5
Rnd 1: K to end of rnd.
Rnd 2: *K6, m1* to end of rnd (16 inc). [112 sts]
Rnd 3: K to end of rnd.
Rnd 4: *K7, m1* to end of rnd (16 inc). [128 sts]
Rnd 5: K to end of rnd.
Rnd 6: *K8, m1* to end of rnd (16 inc). [144 sts]

SIZE 6
Rnd 1: K to end of rnd.
Rnd 2: *K6, m1* to end of rnd (16 inc). [112 sts]
Rnd 3: K to end of rnd.
Rnd 4: *K7, m1* to end of rnd (16 inc). [128 sts]
Rnd 5: K to end of rnd.
Rnd 6: K9, m1, *K5, m1* to last 4 sts, k4 (24 inc). [152 sts]

SIZE 7
Rnd 1: K to end of rnd.
Rnd 2: *K5, m1* to end of rnd (20 inc). [120 sts]
Rnd 3: K to end of rnd.
Rnd 4: *K6, m1* to end of rnd (20 inc). [140 sts]
Rnd 5: K to end of rnd.
Rnd 6: *K5, m1* to end of rnd (28 inc). [168 sts]

SIZE 8
Rnd 1: K to end of rnd.
Rnd 2: *K10, m1* to end of rnd (10 inc). [110 sts]
Rnd 3: K to end of rnd.
Rnd 4: *K5, m1* to end of rnd (22 inc). [132 sts]
Rnd 5: K to end of rnd.
Rnd 6: *K6, m1* to end of rnd (22 inc). [154 sts]
Rnd 7: K to end of rnd.
Rnd 8: *K5, m1* to last 4 sts, k4 (30 inc). [184 sts]

SIZE 9
Rnd 1: K to end of rnd.
Rnd 2: *K10, m1* to end of rnd (10 inc). [110 sts]
Rnd 3: K to end of rnd.
Rnd 4: *K5, m1* to end of rnd (22 inc). [132 sts]
Rnd 5: K to end of rnd.
Rnd 6: *K6, m1* to end of rnd (22 inc). [154 sts]
Rnd 7: K to end of rnd.
Rnd 8: *K4, m1* to last 2 sts, k2 (38 inc). [192 sts]

SIZE 10
Rnd 1: K to end of rnd.
Rnd 2: *K10, m1* to last 4 sts, k4 (10 inc.) [114 sts]
Rnd 3: K to end of rnd.
Rnd 4: *K4, m1* to last 2 sts, k2 (28 inc). [142 sts]
Rnd 5: K to end of rnd.
Rnd 6: K7, m1, *K4, m1* to last 3 sts, k3 (34 inc). [176 sts]
Rnd 7: K to end of rnd.
Rnd 8: K11, m1, *K7, m1* to last 4 sts, k4 (24 inc). [200 sts]

ALL SIZES: Work the rows of the chart shown opposite, making increases as indicated on the chart in the colours stipulated by the key. Before the increases begin, the chart is based on 8 sts, which grows to 20 sts by the end of the increases. Note that the chart repeats 12 (13, 14, 16) 18, 19 [21, 23, 24] 25 times per round.

STITCH COUNT AFTER INCS
After rnd 4, you have 144 (156, 168, 192) 216, 228 [252, 276, 288] 300 sts.
After rnd 15, you have 192 (208, 224, 256) 288, 304 [336, 368, 384] 400 sts.
After rnd 21, you have 240 (260, 280, 320) 360, 380 [420, 460, 480] 500 sts.

SLEEVE SEPARATION
From this point you will cont in mc only. K the first 69 (80, 86, 100) 110, 118 [132, 142, 151] 160 sts for back of body. Transfer the next 51 (50, 54, 60) 70, 72 [78, 88, 89] 90 sts onto scrap yarn for sleeve A. Backwards loop cast-on 13 (14, 16, 16) 16, 18 [16, 18, 19] 20 sts for underarm. Rep over rem sts for front, sleeve B and second underarm. Pm to mark bor. The bor should be on the back of your left shoulder. You have 164 (188, 204, 232) 252, 272 [296, 320, 340] 360 sts on needles.

mc		cc3
cc1	M	m1 - cc1
cc2	M	m1 - cc3

CHEST SHORT-ROW SHAPING (OPTIONAL)

If you have a bigger chest circumference or prefer a fit with more room around your chest area, knit the following section.

SR1 (rs): K 151 (174, 188, 216) 236, 254 [280, 302, 321] 340, w&t.

R2 (ws): P 69 (80, 86, 100) 110, 118 [132, 142, 151] 160, w&t.

SR3 (rs): K 64 (75, 81, 95) 105, 113 [127, 137, 146] 155, w&t.

SR4 (ws): P 59 (70, 76, 90) 100, 108 [122, 132, 141] 150, w&t.

SR5 (rs): K 54 (65, 71, 85) 95, 103 [117, 127, 136] 145, w&t.

SR6 (ws): P 49 (60, 66, 80) 90, 98 [112, 122, 131] 140, w&t.

SR7 (rs): K 44 (55, 61, 75) 85, 93 [107, 117, 126] 135, w&t.

SR8 (ws): P 39 (50, 56, 70) 80, 88 [102, 112, 121, 130, w&t.

SR9 (rs): K – (–, –, 65) 75, 83 [97, 107, 116] 125, w&t.

SR10 (ws): P – (–, –, 60) 70, 78 [92, 102, 111] 120, w&t.

SR11 (rs): K – (–, –, –) –, – [–, 97, 106] 115, w&t.

SR12 (ws): P – (–, –, –) –, – [–, 92, 101] 110, w&t.

With rs facing, k to marker, picking up wraps and knitting them together with the wrapped sts as you go.

K 1 rnd, picking up remaining wraps as you go.

BODY

There are two options for body length – cropped or regular. If you are shorter or prefer a slightly cropped jumper, knit the section below labelled "cropped body". If you are taller or prefer a longer jumper, knit the section below labelled "regular body".

CROPPED BODY

Cont working in the rnd in st st until work measures 15.5 (15.5, 15.5, 15.5) 15.5, 15.5 [15.5, 15.5, 15.5] 15.5cm/6 (6, 6, 6) 6, 6 [6, 6, 6]in from underarm.

REGULAR BODY

Cont working in the rnd in st st until work measures 28 (30.5, 33, 35.5) 38.5, 41 [42, 44, 44] 46cm/11 (12, 13, 14) 15¼, 16¼ [16½, 17¼, 17¼] 18in from underarm.

HEM

Work *k1, p1* ribbing until hem measures 5cm/2in.
Bind off loosely.

SLEEVES

Transfer the held sts for one sleeve from scrap yarn onto working needle, pick up an additional 13 (14, 16, 16) 16, 18 [16, 18, 19] 20 sts from underarm. Working in mc, k the next 58 (57, 62, 68) 78, 81 [86, 97, 99] 100 sts, pm to mark bor. You have a total of 64 (64, 70, 76) 86, 90 [94, 106, 108] 110 sts.

SLEEVE LENGTHS

There are two sleeve length options – a shorter version (bracelet) and a longer version (full). Cont to your preferred length section.

SHORTER SLEEVE – BRACELET

Rnd 1: K to end of rnd.
Dec rnd: *K1, ssk, k to last 3 sts, k2tog, k1* (2 sts dec).
Work dec rnd every 10 (14, 10, 8) 7, 6 [5, 4, 4] 4 rnds for a total of 10 (8, 11, 14) 17, 19 [21, 27, 28] 29 times. After final dec, you have 44 (48, 48, 48) 52, 52 [52, 52, 52] 52 sts.
Cont in st st until sleeve measures 43.5 (44.5, 44.5, 46) 46, 47 [47, 48.5, 48.5] 48.5cm/17¼ (17½, 17½, 18) 18, 18½ [18½, 19, 19] 19in from underarm. Cont to cuff section.

LONGER SLEEVE – FULL

Rnd 1: K to end of rnd.
Dec rnd: *K1, ssk, k to last 3 sts, k2tog, k1* (2 sts dec).
Work dec rnd every 11 (14, 10, 8) 7, 7 [6, 5, 5] 5 rnds for a total of 10 (8, 11, 14) 17, 19 [21, 27, 28] 29 times. After final dec, you have 44 (48, 48, 48) 52, 52 [52, 52, 52] 52 sts.
Cont in st st until sleeve measures 45.5 (46.5, 47, 48.5) 51, 52 [53.5, 53.5, 54.5] 55cm/18 (18¼, 18½, 19) 20, 20½ [21, 21, 21½] 21¾in from underarm. Cont to cuff section.

CUFF

Using mc, work *k1, p1* ribbing until cuff measures 5cm/2in. Bind off loosely.

FINISHING

Weave in all ends. Wet block to measurements.

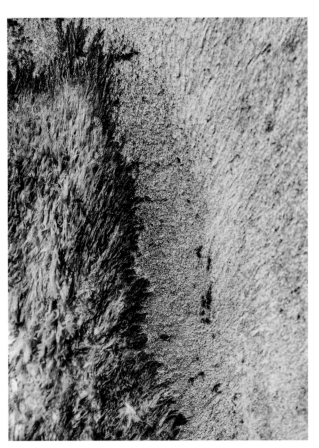

FJORD JUMPER

Fjord is a design that captures the colours of the granite mountains while they glisten in the snow and sun. While cruising down the Arctic fjords, you can catch a glimpse of the vast mountain range and its impressive peaks.

NOTES

This jumper pattern is unisex, has a boxy fit, and comes in ten adult sizes. There are two options for body length options – cropped and regular. Because the jumper is knitted top-down, you can easily customize the length by stopping before or continuing after the recommended body length measurements. There are also two sleeve length options – bracelet length and full length – so you can customize the jumper to fit you best. As each body is unique, please remember that the pattern serves as a guide. Feel free to modify any lengths or to fit your own body and arms. The colourwork chart is read from right to left, bottom to top. The intended ease is about 5cm/2in to 10cm/4in. Remember to swatch to check gauge and size up or down with needles as needed.

CONSTRUCTION

This jumper is knitted top-down and in the round. You begin at the neck, which is followed by a seamless colourwork round yoke that expands in width with regular increases.

There is optional short-row shaping to raise the back of the neck and also to create more room about the chest area, to suit your preferences. Once the yoke is complete, you separate for the sleeves to create armholes and then continue with the body. When you have knitted the body you return to the reserved stitches you separated for the sleeves. The tapered sleeves are knitted top-down and in the round as well.

SIZES

1 (2, 3, 4) 5, 6 [7, 8, 9] 10

HOW TO PICK A SIZE

For a comfortable fit, this jumper should be worn with a positive ease of 5cm/2in to 10cm/4in. Measure the widest section of your chest with a measuring tape. For example, your chest measurement is 100cm/39½in. If you prefer less positive ease, you should pick size 4 for a positive ease of 5cm/2in. If you prefer more positive ease, you should pick size 5 for a positive ease of 15cm/6in.

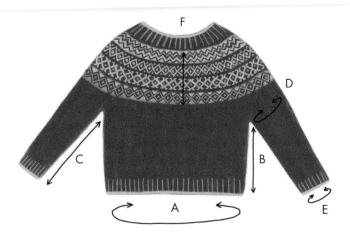

MEASUREMENTS

A: CHEST CIRCUMFERENCE
cm: 76 (86, 95, 105) 115, 125 [135, 145, 155] 165
in: 30 (33¾, 37½, 41¼) 45¼, 49¼ [53¼, 57, 61] 65

B1: SIDE LENGTH – CROPPED
cm: 21.5 (22, 22, 22) 22, 22 [22, 22, 22] 22
in: 8½ (8¾, 8¾, 8¾) 8¾, 8¾ [8¾, 8¾, 8¾] 8¾

B2: SIDE LENGTH – REGULAR
cm: 34.5 (37, 39.5, 42) 45, 47.5 [48.5, 50.5, 50.5] 52.5
in: 13½ (14½, 15½, 16½) 17¾, 18¾ [19, 20, 20] 20¾

C1: SLEEVE LENGTH – BRACELET
cm: 44.5 (45.5, 45.5, 47) 47, 48 [48, 49.5, 49.5] 49.5
in: 17½ (18, 18, 18½) 18½, 19 [19, 19¼, 19¼] 19½

C2: SLEEVE LENGTH – FULL
cm: 46.5 (47.5, 48, 50.5) 52.5, 53 [54.5, 54.5, 55.5] 56
in: 18¼ (18¾, 19, 20) 20¾, 21 [21½, 21½, 21¾] 22

D: UPPER ARM
cm: 29 (30, 32, 35) 39, 41 [42.5, 48, 49] 50
in: 11½ (11¾, 12½, 13¾) 15¼, 16¼ [16¾, 19, 19¼] 19¾

E: WRIST CIRCUMFERENCE
cm: 20.5 (21, 21.5, 22) 23, 23 [23.5, 23.5, 23.5] 24.5
in: 8 (8¼, 8½, 8¾) 9, 9 [9¼, 9¼, 9¼] 9¾

F: YOKE DEPTH
cm: 23.5 (24, 24.5, 24.5) 25.5, 25.5 [25.5, 26.5, 26.5] 26.5
in: 9¼ (9½, 9¾, 9¾) 10, 10 [10, 10½, 10½] 10½

YARN
Sonder Yarn Co. Sunday Morning (75% Bluefaced Leicester, 25% Masham, DK (light worsted) weight)

SAMPLE 1
mc – Dirty Weekend
cc – Offline

SAMPLE 2
mc – Offline
cc – Crossword

YARDAGE
METRES – CROPPED
mc: 603 (638, 708, 774) 856, 914 [964, 1053, 1102] 1157
cc: 99 (103, 118, 128) 143, 153 [162, 177, 187] 198

YARDS – CROPPED
mc: 660 (698, 775, 847) 937, 1000 [1055, 1152, 1206] 1266
cc: 110 (115, 130, 140) 157, 168 [177, 195, 205] 217

METRES – REGULAR
mc: 728 (799, 921, 1037) 1200, 1319 [1426, 1571, 1659] 1805
cc: 99 (103, 118, 128) 143, 153 [162, 177, 187] 198

YARDS – REGULAR
mc: 797 (874, 1008, 1135) 1313, 1443 [1560, 1719, 1815] 1975
cc: 109 (113, 130, 140) 157, 168 [178, 194, 205] 217

SAMPLE 1   SAMPLE 2

GAUGE
24 sts x 26 rnds = 10cm/4in in colourwork sts
22 sts x 30 rnds = 10cm/4in in stockinette st

NEEDLES
Size 3.5 mm/US4 or size necessary to obtain gauge. Use fixed circular knitting needles or cables for interchangeable needles in the following lengths:
40cm/16in
60cm/24in
80cm/32in

NOTIONS
Stitch markers
Tapestry needle
Scrap yarn

BEGIN PATTERN – NECK
Using 3.5mm/US4 needles and cc, co 92 (92, 92, 98) 104, 104 [110, 110, 110] 114 sts using the long-tail cast-on method. Join to work in the rnd and pm to mark bor (at left back shoulder). Attach mc. Using mc, k 1 rnd. Cont with mc, work *k1, p1* ribbing until work measures 4cm/1.5in from co edge. Cut cc.

NECK SHORT-ROW SHAPING
K 1 rnd.
Begin short-row shaping.
SR1 (rs): K 46 (46, 46, 49) 52, 52 [55, 55, 55] 57, w&t.
SR2 (ws): P 69 (69, 69, 74) 78, 78 [83, 83, 83] 86, w&t.
SR3 (rs): K 64 (64, 64, 69) 73, 73 [78, 78, 78] 81, w&t.
SR4 (ws): P 59 (59, 59, 64) 68, 68 [73, 73, 73] 76, w&t.
SR5 (rs): K 54 (54, 54, 59) 63, 63 [68, 68, 68] 71, w&t.
SR6 (ws): P 49 (49, 49, 54) 58, 58 [63, 63, 63] 66, w&t.
SR7 (rs): K – (–, –, 49) 53, 53 [58, 58, 58] 61, w&t.
SR8 (ws): P – (–, –, 44) 48, 48 [53, 53, 53] 56, w&t.
With rs facing, k to marker, picking up wraps and knitting them together with the wrapped sts as you go.
K 1 rnd, picking up remaining wraps as you go.

YOKE
Before working the chart, knit the following inc rounds to set up the yoke. Refer to the section correlating with your chosen size. As the width of the work expands while you work on the yoke, switch to longer circular needles (or cables, if you are using interchangeable needles) for your comfort.

SIZE 1
Rnd 1: K to end of rnd.
Rnd 2: K10, m1, *k6, m1* to last 4 sts, k4 (14 inc). [106]
Rnd 3: K to end of rnd.
Rnd 4: K11, m1, *k7, m1* to last 4 sts, k4 (14 inc). [120]

SIZE 2
Rnd 1: K to end of rnd.
Rnd 2: K10, m1, *k6, m1* to last 4 sts, k4 (14 inc). [106 sts]
Rnd 3: K to end of rnd.
Rnd 4: *K5, m1* to last 6 sts, k6 (20 inc). [126 sts]

SIZE 3
Rnd 1: K to end of rnd.
Rnd 2: *K9, m1* to last 2 sts, k2 (10 inc). [102 sts]
Rnd 3: K to end of rnd.
Rnd 4: *K5, m1* to last 2 sts, k2 (20 inc). [122 sts]
Rnd 5: K to end of rnd.
Rnd 6: K11, m1, *k5, m1* to last 6 sts, k6 (22 inc). [144 sts]

SIZE 4
Rnd 1: K to end of rnd.
Rnd 2: *K7, m1* to end of rnd (14 inc). [112 sts]
Rnd 3: K to end of rnd.
Rnd 4: *K5, m1* to last 2 sts, k2 (22 inc). [134 sts]
Rnd 5: K to end of rnd.
Rnd 6: *K6, m1* to last 2 sts, k2 (22 inc). [156 sts]

SIZE 5
Rnd 1: K to end of rnd.
Rnd 2: K10, m1, *k6, m1* to last 4 sts, k4 (16 inc). [120 sts]
Rnd 3: K to end of rnd.
Rnd 4: K8, m1, *k4, m1* to last 4 sts, k4 (28 inc). [148 sts]
Rnd 5: K to end of rnd.
Rnd 6: K14, m1, *k5, m1* to last 9 sts, k9 (26 inc). [174 sts]

SIZE 6
Rnd 1: K to end of rnd.
Rnd 2: K8, m1, *K4, m1* to last 4 sts, k4 (24 inc). [128 sts]
Rnd 3: K to end of rnd.
Rnd 4: *K4, m1* to end of rnd (32 inc). [160 sts]
Rnd 5: K to end of rnd.
Rnd 6: *K6, m1* to last 4 sts, k4 (26 inc). [186 sts]

SIZE 7

Rnd 1: K to end of rnd.
Rnd 2: K7, m1, *K4, m1* to last 3 sts, k3 (26 inc). [136 sts]
Rnd 3: K to end of rnd.
Rnd 4: *K4, m1* to end of rnd (34 inc). [170 sts]
Rnd 5: K to end of rnd.
Rnd 6: *K6, m1* to last 2 sts, k2 (28 inc). [198 sts]

SIZE 8

Rnd 1: K to end of rnd.
Rnd 2: *K10, m1* to end of rnd (11 inc). [121 sts]
Rnd 3: K to end of rnd.
Rnd 4: *K4, m1* to last sts, k1 (30 inc). [151 sts]
Rnd 5: K to end of rnd.
Rnd 6: K8, m1, *K4, m1* to last 3 sts, k3 (36 inc). [187 sts]
Rnd 7: K to end of rnd.
Rnd 8: K12, m1, *K6, m1* to last 7 sts, k7 (29 inc). [216 sts]

SIZE 9

Rnd 1: K to end of rnd.
Rnd 2: *K5, m1* to end of rnd (22 inc). [132 sts]
Rnd 3: K to end of rnd.
Rnd 4: K10, m1, *K4, m1* to last 6 sts, k6 (30 inc). [162 sts]
Rnd 5: K to end of rnd.
Rnd 6: K11, m1, *K5, m1* to last 6 sts, k6 (30 inc). [192 sts]
Rnd 7: K to end of rnd.
Rnd 8: K11, m1, *K5, m1* to last 6 sts, k6 (36 inc). [228 sts]

SIZE 10

Rnd 1: K to end of rnd.
Rnd 2: K14, m1, *K4, m1* to last 8 sts, k8 (24 inc). [138 sts]
Rnd 3: K to end of rnd.
Rnd 4: *K4, m1* to last 2 sts, k2 (34 inc). [172 sts]
Rnd 5: K to end of rnd.
Rnd 6: *K5, m1* to last 2 sts, k2 (34 inc). [206 sts]
Rnd 7: K to end of rnd.
Rnd 8: *K6, m1* to last 2 sts, k2 (34 inc). [240 sts]

ALL SIZES: Work the rows of the chart shown opposite, making increases as indicated on the chart in the colours stipulated by the key. Before the increases begin, the chart is based on 6 sts, which grows to 14 sts by the end of the increases. Note that the chart repeats 20 (21, 24, 26) 29, 31, [33, 36, 38] 40 times per round.

mc

cc

M m1 - mc

M m1 - cc

no stitch

STITCH COUNT AFTER INCS

After rnd 2, you have 160 (168, 192, 208) 232, 248 [264, 288, 304] 320 sts.

After rnd 12, you have 200 (210, 240, 260) 290, 310 [330, 360, 380] 400 sts.

After rnd 14 you have 240 (252, 288, 312) 348, 372 [396, 432, 456] 480 sts.

After rnd 44, you have 280 (294, 336, 364) 406, 434 [462, 504, 532] 560 sts.

SLEEVE SEPARATION

Using mc, k the first 81 (89, 104, 113) 123, 134 [143, 154, 167] 180 sts for back of body. Transfer the next 59 (58, 64, 69) 80, 83 [88, 98, 99] 100 sts onto scrap yarn for sleeve A. Backwards-loop cast-on 11 (12, 12, 13) 14, 15 [16, 18, 19] 20 sts for underarm. Rep over rem sts for front, sleeve B and second underarm. Pm to mark bor. The bor should be on the back of your left shoulder. You have 184 (202, 232, 252) 274, 298 [318, 344, 372] 400 sts on needles.

CHEST SHORT-ROW SHAPING (OPTIONAL)

If you have a bigger chest circumference or prefer a fit with more room around your chest area, knit the following section.
SR1 (rs): K 173 (190, 220, 239) 260, 283 [302, 326, 353] 380, w&t.
SR2 (ws): P 81, 89, 104, 113) 123, 134 [143, 154, 167] 180, w&t.
SR3 (rs): K 76 (84, 99, 108) 118, 129 [138, 149, 162] 175, w&t.
SR4 (ws): P 71 (79, 94, 103) 113, 124 [133, 144, 157] 170, w&t.
SR5 (rs): K 66 (74, 89, 98) 108, 119 [128, 139, 152] 165, w&t.
SR6 (ws): P 61 (69, 84, 93) 103, 114 [123, 134, 147] 160, w&t.
SR7 (rs): K 56 (64, 79, 88) 98, 109 [118, 129, 142] 155, w&t.
SR8 (ws): P 51 (59, 74, 83) 93, 104 [113, 124, 137] 150, w&t.
SR9 (rs): K – (–, –, 78) 88, 99 [108, 119, 132] 145, w&t.
SR10 (ws): P – (–, –, 73) 83, 94 [103, 114, 127] 140, w&t.
SR11 (rs): K – (–, –, –) –, – [–, 109, 122] 135, w&t.
SR12 (ws): P – (–, –, –) –, – [–, 104, 117] 130, w&t.
With rs facing, k to marker, picking up wraps and knitting them together with the wrapped sts as you go.
K 1 round, picking up remaining wraps.

BODY

There are two options for body length – cropped or regular. If you are shorter or prefer a cropped jumper, knit the section below labelled "cropped body". If you are taller or prefer a longer jumper, knit the section below labelled "regular body".

CROPPED BODY

Cont working in the rnd in st st until work measures 17.5 (18, 18, 18) 18, 18 [18, 18, 18] 18cm/6¾ (7, 7, 7) 7, 7 [7, 7, 7] 7in from underarm.

REGULAR BODY

Cont working in the rnd in st st until work measures 30.5 (33, 35.5, 38) 41, 43.5 [44.5, 46.5, 46.5] 48.5cm/12 (13, 14, 15) 16¼, 17¼ [17½, 18¼, 18¼] 19in from underarm.

HEM

Work *k1, p1* ribbing until hem measures approx 4cm/1½in. Knit 1 rnd. Cut mc, attach cc. Bind off loosely with cc.

SLEEVES

Transfer held sts for one sleeve from scrap yarn needle to working needle, pick up an additional 11 (12, 12, 13) 14, 15 [16, 18, 19] 20 sts from underarm. K the next 64 (64, 70, 76) 87, 90 [96, 107, 108] 110 sts, pm to mark bor. You have a total of 70 (70, 76, 82) 94, 98 [104, 116, 118] 120 sts.

SLEEVE LENGTHS

There are two sleeve length options – a shorter version (bracelet) and a longer version (full). Cont to your preferred length section.

SHORTER SLEEVE – BRACELET

Rnd 1: Using mc, k to end of rnd.
Dec rnd: *K1, ssk, k to last 3 sts, k2tog, k1* (2 sts dec).

Work dec rnd every 7 (7, 7, 6) 5, 4 [4, 3, 3] 3 rnds for a total of 10 (10, 12, 15) 19, 21 [24, 30, 31] 31 times. After final dec, you have 50 (50, 52, 52) 56, 56 [56, 56, 56] 58 sts. Cont in st st until sleeve measures 40.5 (42, 42, 43) 43, 44 [44, 45.5, 45.5] 45.5cm/16 (16½, 16½, 17) 17, 17¼ [17¼, 18, 18] 18in from underarm. Cont to cuff section.

LONGER SLEEVE – FULL
Rnd 1: Using mc, k all sts to end of rnd.
Dec rnd: *K1, ssk, k to last 3 sts, k2tog, k1* (2 sts dec).

Work dec rnd every 10 (10, 8, 7) 6, 5 [5, 4, 4] 4 rnds for a total of 10 (10, 12, 15) 19, 21 [24, 30, 31] 31 times. After final dec, you have 50 (50, 52, 52) 56, 56 [56, 56, 56] 58 sts. Cont in st st until sleeve measures 42.5 (43.5, 44, 46.5) 48.5, 49 [50.5, 50.5, 51.5] 52cm/16¾ (17¼, 17¼, 18¼) 19, 19¼ [20, 20, 20¼] 20½in from underarm. Cont to cuff section.

CUFF
Work *k1, p1* ribbing until cuff measures approx 4cm/1½in.
K 1 rnd.
Cut mc, attach cc. Bind off loosely with cc.

FINISHING
Weave in all ends. Wet block to measurements.

FJORD HAT

NOTES

The colourwork chart is read from bottom to top and right to left. Please swatch to ensure you have the right gauge before beginning. Stranded colourwork might affect your usual gauge so please adjust needle size as needed.

CONSTRUCTION

This hat is knitted from bottom-up and in the round. It features a colourwork motif throughout. The crown is created through decrease intervals. You can choose from folded or single-brim options.

SIZES

1 (2) 3

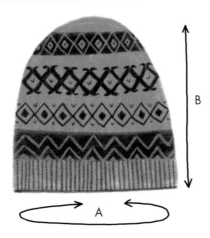

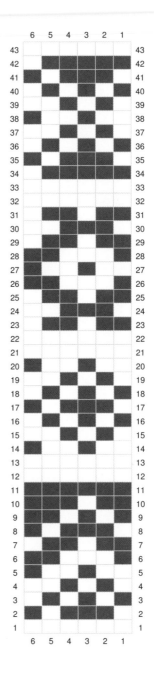

FINISHED MEASUREMENTS
A: HEAD CIRCUMFERENCE
cm: 49 (52) 55
in: 19¼ (20½) 21¾

B: HEIGHT
cm: 23 (23) 23
in: 9 (9) 9

YARN
Sonder Yarn Co. Sunday Morning (75% Bluefaced Leicester, 25% Masham, DK (light worsted) weight)

SAMPLE 1
Colour A – Offline
Colour B – Crossword

SAMPLE 2
Colour A – Dirty Weekend
Colour B – Offline

YARDAGE
COLOUR A
Metres: 180 (200) 220
Yards: 197 (219) 241

COLOUR B
Metres: 102 (107) 112
Yards: 112 (117) 123

GAUGE
28 sts and 28.5 rnds = 10cm/4in in colourwork sts

colour A

colour B

NEEDLES
3.5mm (US4) needles or size necessary to obtain gauge. Use 40cm/16in fixed or interchangeable circular needles and DPNs.

NOTIONS
Stitch markers
Tapestry needle

SAMPLE 1

SAMPLE 2

BEGIN PATTERN – BRIM

With colour B, co 120 (132, 144) sts. Join in the rnd, pm to mark bor. Attach colour A, k1 rnd. Work *k1, p1* ribbing until work measures:

Folded brim: 8 (8) 8cm/3¼ (3¼) 3¼in from co edge. Fold brim in half. Cut cc.

Single brim: 4 (4) 4 cm/1½ (1½) 1½in from co edge. Cut cc.

HAT

Work the rows of the chart shown opposite. Note that the chart repeats 20 (22) 24 times per round.

DECS RNDS

Switch to DPNs as needed during dec rnds.

Rnd 1: *K10, k2tog* to end of rnd. You have 110 (121) 132 sts.
Rnd 2: *K9, k2tog* to end of rnd. You have 100 (110) 120 sts.
Rnd 3: *K8, k2tog* to end of rnd. You have 90 (99) 108 sts.

Rnd 4: *K7, k2tog* to end of rnd. You have 80 (88) 96 sts.
Rnd 5: *K6, k2tog* to end of rnd. You have 70 (77) 84 sts.
Rnd 6: *K5, k2tog* to end of rnd. You have 60 (66) 72 sts.
Rnd 7: *K4, k2tog* to end of rnd. You have 50 (55) 60 sts.
Rnd 8: *K3, k2tog* to end of rnd. You have 40 (44) 48 sts.
Rnd 9: *K2, k2tog* to end of rnd. You have 30 (33) 36 sts.
Rnd 10: *K1, k2tog* to end of rnd. You have 20 (22) 24 sts.
Rnd 11: *K2tog* to end of rnd. You have 10 (11) 12 sts.

FINISHING

Break working yarn and thread tapestry needle through. Draw through the rem 10 (11) 12 sts going around all sts twice. Pull up tightly and fasten securely on the inside.

Weave in ends and wet block to measurements.

BAFFIN JUMPER

Located on the cusp of the Arctic Circle, Baffin Island is the largest island in Canada. Baffin spans well above the Arctic Circle and is home to the world's most remote and majestic snow-capped mountains and alpine glaciers. This design is inspired by the iconic Baffin granite peaks and their legends.

NOTES

This jumper pattern is unisex, has a boxy fit, and comes in ten adult sizes. There are two options for body length – cropped and regular. Because the jumper is knitted top-down, you can easily customize the length by stopping before or continuing after the recommended body length measurements. As each body is unique, please remember that the pattern serves as a guide. Feel free to modify any lengths to fit your own body. The colourwork charts are read from right to left, bottom to top. The intended positive ease is about 11.5cm/4½in to 24cm/9½in. Remember to swatch, check gauge, and size up or down with needles as needed.

CONSTRUCTION

This jumper is knitted top-down and in the round. You begin at the neck, which is followed by a seamless colourwork round yoke that expands in width with regular increases. Once the yoke is complete, you separate for the sleeves to create armholes and then continue with the body. There is optional short-row shaping to create more room about the chest area. When you have knitted the body you return to the reserved stitches you separated for the sleeves. The sleeves are knitted top-down and in the round as well.

SIZES

1 (2, 3, 4) 5, 6 [7, 8, 9] 10

HOW TO PICK A SIZE

For a comfortable fit, this jumper should be worn with a positive ease of 11.5cm/4½in to 24cm/9½in. Measure the widest section of your chest with a measuring tape. For example, your chest measurement is 90cm/35½in. If you prefer less positive ease, you should pick size 3 for a positive ease of 12cm/4¾in. If you prefer more positive ease, you should pick size 4 for a positive ease of 23cm/9in.

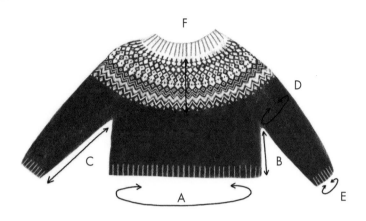

MEASUREMENTS

A: CHEST CIRCUMFERENCE
cm: 82 (92.5, 102, 113) 122.5, 132.5 [145, 153, 162] 173.5
in: 32¼ (36½, 40¼, 44½) 48¼, 52¼ [57, 60¼, 63¾] 68¼

B1: SIDE LENGTH – SHORT
cm: 21.5 (22, 22, 22) 22, 22 [22, 22, 22] 22
in: 8½ (8¾, 8¾, 8¾) 8¾, 8¾ [8¾, 8¾, 8¾] 8¾

B2: SIDE LENGTH – LONG
cm: 34.5 (37, 39.5, 42) 45, 47.5 [48.5, 50.5, 50.5] 52.5
in: 13½ (14½, 15½, 16½) 17¾, 18¾ [19, 20, 20] 20¾

C: SLEEVE LENGTH
cm: 45.5 (47, 47.5, 48.5) 49, 50 [51, 51.5, 52.5] 53.5
in: 18 (18½, 18¾, 19) 19¼, 19¾ [20, 20¼, 20¾] 21

D: UPPER ARM
cm: 28.5 (31, 34.5, 37.5) 40, 40.5 [44, 46.5, 49] 52.5
in: 11¼ (12¼, 13½, 14¾) 15¾, 16 [17¼, 18¼, 19¼] 20¾

E: WRIST CIRCUMFERENCE
cm: 19.5 (21, 22, 23) 24, 26 [26.5, 26.5, 29] 29
in: 7¾ (8¼, 8¾, 9) 9½, 10¼ [10½, 10½, 11½] 11½

F: YOKE DEPTH
cm: 20.5 (21, 21.5, 23) 23, 23.5 [25, 25.5, 26] 26.5
in: 8 (8¼, 8½, 9) 9, 9¼ [9¾, 10, 10¼] 10½

YARN
Biches & Bûches Le Petit Lambswool (100% lambswool, fingering (4ply) weight)
mc – Dark gold
cc – White

YARDAGE
METRES – CROPPED
mc: 760 (835, 908, 1017) 1109, 1174 [1255, 1358, 1429] 1495
cc: 120 (130, 143, 160) 176, 186 [199, 215, 229] 239

YARDS – CROPPED
mc: 832 (914, 993, 1113) 1213, 1284 [1373, 1486, 1563] 1635
cc: 132 (143, 157, 175) 193, 204 [218, 236, 251] 262

METRES – REGULAR
mc: 937 (1053, 1181, 1360) 1561, 1699 [1843, 2025, 2146] 2321
cc: 120 (130, 143, 160) 176, 186 [199, 215, 229] 239

YARDS – REGULAR
mc: 1025 (1152, 1292, 1488) 1708, 1859 [2016, 2215, 2347] 2539
cc: 132 (143, 157, 175) 193, 204 [218, 236, 251] 262

GAUGE
24 sts x 26 rnds = 10cm/4in in colourwork sts
25 sts x 27 rnds = 10cm/4in in stockinette st

NEEDLES
Size 3.5mm/US4 circular needles or size necessary to obtain gauge. Use fixed circular knitting needles or cables for interchangeable needles in the following lengths:
40cm/16in
60cm/24in
80cm/32in

NOTIONS
Stitch markers
Tapestry needle
Scrap yarn

BEGIN PATTERN – NECK
Using 3.5mm/US4 needles and cc, co 88 (92, 98, 110) 116, 120 [122, 128, 132] 134 sts using your preferred stretchy cast-on technique. Join in the rnd and pm to mark bor.

Work *k1, p1* ribbing until work measures 5cm/2in from co edge.

YOKE
Before working the chart, knit the following inc rounds to set up the yoke. Refer to the section correlating with your chosen size. As the width of the work expands while you work on the yoke, switch to longer circular needles (or cables, if you are using interchangeable needles) for your comfort.

SIZE 1
Rnd 1–3: K to end of rnd. [88 sts]

SIZE 2
Rnd 1: K to end of rnd.
Rnd 2: *K23, m1* to end of rnd (4 sts inc). [96 sts]
Rnd 3: K to end of rnd.

SIZE 3
Rnd 1: K to end of rnd.
Rnd 2: *K16, m1* to last 2 sts, k2 (6 sts inc). [104 sts]
Rnd 3: K to end of rnd.

SIZE 4
Rnd 1: K to end of rnd.
Rnd 2: *K18, m1* to last 2 sts, k2 (6 sts inc). [116 sts]
Rnd 3: K to end of rnd.

SIZE 5
Rnd 1: K to end of rnd.
Rnd 2: *K14, m1* to last 4 sts (8 sts inc). [124 sts]
Rnd 3: K to end of rnd.

SIZE 6
Rnd 1: K to end of rnd.
Rnd 2: *K10, m1* to end (12 sts inc). [132 sts]
Rnd 3: K to end of rnd.

SIZE 7
Rnd 1: K to end of rnd.
Rnd 2: *K5, m1, k6, m1* to last st, k1 (22 sts inc). [144 sts]
Rnd 3: K to end of rnd.

SIZE 8
Rnd 1: K to end of rnd.
Rnd 2: *K9, m1* to last 2 sts, k2 (14 sts inc). [142 sts]
Rnd 3: K to end of rnd.
Rnd 4: *K14, m1* to last 2 sts, k2 (10 sts inc). [152 sts]

SIZE 9
Rnd 1: K to end of rnd.
Rnd 2: *K8, m1* to last 4 sts, k4 (16 sts inc). [148 sts]
Rnd 3: K to end of rnd.
Rnd 4: *K12, m1* to last 4 sts, k4 (12 sts inc). [160 sts]

SIZE 10
Rnd 1: K to end of rnd.
Rnd 2: *K6, m1* to last 8 sts, k8 (21 sts inc). [155 sts]
Rnd 3: K to end of rnd.
Rnd 4: *K9, m1* to last 2 sts, k2 (17 sts inc). [172 sts]

ALL SIZES: Work the rows of the chart shown opposite, making increases as indicated on the chart in the colours stipulated by the key. Before the increases begin, the chart is based on 4 sts, which grows to 14 sts by the end of the increases. Note that the chart repeats 22 (24, 26, 29) 31, 33 [36, 38, 40] 43 times per round.

STITCH COUNT AFTER INCS
After rnd 2, you have 132 (144, 156, 174) 186, 198 [216, 228, 240] 258 sts.
After rnd 5, you have 176 (192, 208, 232) 248, 264 [288, 304, 320] 344 sts.
After rnd 11, you have 220 (240, 260, 290) 310, 330 [360, 380, 400] 430 sts.

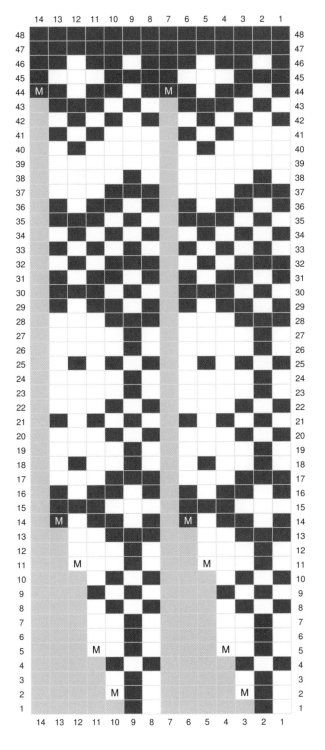

After rnd 14, you have 264 (288, 312, 348) 372, 396 [432, 456, 480] 516 sts.
After rnd 44, you have 308 (336, 364, 406) 434, 462 [504, 532, 560] 602 sts.

Using mc, cont in st st until yoke measures 20.5 (21, 21.5, 23) 23, 23.5 [25, 25.5, 26] 26.5cm/8 (8¼, 8½, 9) 9, 9¼ [9¾, 10, 10¼] 10½in from ribbing or desired length to underarm.

SLEEVE SEPARATION

K the first 92 (103, 112, 125) 135, 147 [161, 170, 179] 192 sts for back of body. Place the next 62 (65, 70, 78) 82, 84 [91, 96, 101] 109 sts on stitch holder or scrap yarn for sleeve A. Backwards loop cast-on 9 (11, 14, 14) 16, 16 [17, 18, 20] 21 sts for underarm. Rep for front, sleeve B and second underarm over rem sts. Pm to mark bor. The bor should be on the back of your left shoulder. You have 202 (228, 252, 278) 302, 326 [356, 376, 398] 426 sts on needles.

CHEST SHORT-ROW SHAPING (OPTIONAL)

If you have a bigger chest circumference or prefer a fit with more room around your chest area, knit the following section.
SR1 (rs): K 193 (217, 238, 264) 286, 310 [339, 358, 378] 405 sts, w&t.
SR2 (ws): P 91 (102, 111, 124) 134, 146 [160, 169, 178] 191 sts, w&t.
SR3 (rs): K 86 (97, 106, 119) 129, 141 [155, 164, 173] 186 sts, w&t.
SR4 (ws): P 81 (92, 101, 114) 124, 136 [150, 159, 168] 181 sts, w&t.
SR5 (rs): K 76 (87, 96, 109) 119, 131 [145, 154, 163] 176 sts, w&t.
SR6 (ws): P 71 (82, 91, 104) 114, 126 [140, 149, 158] 171 sts, w&t.
SR7 (rs): K 66 (77, 86, 99) 109, 121 [135, 144, 153] 166 sts, w&t.
SR8 (ws): P 61 (72, 81, 94) 104, 116 [130, 139, 148] 161 sts, w&t.
With rs facing, k to marker, picking up wraps and knitting them together with the wrapped sts as you go.
K 1 rnd, picking up remaining wraps.

■ mc
□ cc
■ M m1 - mc
M m1 - cc
▨ no stitch

BODY

There are two options for body length – cropped or regular. If you are shorter or prefer a cropped jumper, knit the section below labelled "cropped body". If you are taller or prefer a longer jumper, knit the section below labelled "regular body".

CROPPED BODY

Cont working in the rnd in st st until work measures 16.5 (17, 17, 17) 17, 17 [17, 17, 17] 17cm/6½ (6¾, 6¾, 6¾) 6¾, 6¾ [6¾, 6¾, 6¾] 6¾in from underarm.

REGULAR BODY

Cont working in the rnd in st st until work measures 29.5 (32, 34.5, 37) 40, 42.5 [43.5, 45.5, 45.5] 47.5cm/ 11½ (12½, 13½, 14½) 15¾, 16¾, [17, 18, 18] 18¾in from underarm.

HEM

Using mc, work *k1, p1* ribbing until hem measures 5cm/2in. Bind off loosely.

SLEEVES

Transfer 62 (65, 70, 78) 82, 84 [91, 96, 101] 109 held sleeve sts to needle. With rs facing, beginning at the center of the underarm, pick up and k 4 (5, 7, 7) 8, 8 [8, 9, 9] 10 sts, knit to end of sleeve sts, pick up and k 4 (6, 7, 7) 8, 8 [9, 9, 10] 11 sts, pm for bor and join for working in the rnd. You have a total of 70 (76, 84, 92) 98, 100 [108, 114, 120] 130 sts.

SLEEVE DECREASES

Rnd 1: K 1 rnd.
Dec rnd: K1, k2tog, k to last 3 sts, SSK, k1 (2 sts dec).

Work dec rnd every 12 (12, 10, 8) 8, 8 [8, 6, 6] 6 rnds a further 5 (2, 2, 7) 5, 10 [2, 17, 14] 9 times.

Next, work dec rnd every 10 (10, 8, 6) 6, 6 [6, 4, 4], 4 rnds a further 5 (9, 12, 10) 13, 7 [18, 6, 9] 19 times. After final dec row, you have 48 (52, 54, 56) 60, 64 [66, 66, 72] 72 sts. Cont in st st until sleeve measures 45.5 (47, 47.5, 48.5) 49, 50 [51, 51.5, 52.5] 53.5cm/18 (18½, 18¾, 19) 19¼, 19¾ [20, 20¼, 20¾] 21in from underarm or 4cm/1½in less than desired length. Cont to cuff section

CUFF

Using mc, work *k1, p1* ribbing until cuff measures 5cm/2in. Bind off loosely.

FINISHING

Weave in all ends. Wet block to measurements.

PINGO JUMPER

Pingos are little dome-shaped ice hills surrounded by permafrost in the Arctic. These cute little formations have found their way into this design.

NOTES

This jumper pattern is unisex, has a boxy fit, and comes in ten adult sizes. There are two options for body length – cropped and regular. Because the jumper is knitted top-down, you can easily customize the length by stopping before or continuing after the recommended body length measurements. There are also two sleeve length options – bracelet length and full length – so you can customize the jumper to fit you best. As each body is unique, please remember that the pattern serves as a guide. Feel free to modify any lengths to fit your own body and arms. The colourwork chart is read from right to left, bottom to top. The intended positive ease is about 5cm/2in to 10cm/4in. This jumper is knitted with one strand of mohair and one strand of fingering (4 ply) weight yarn held together. Remember to swatch, check gauge, and size needles up or down as needed.

CONSTRUCTION

This jumper is knitted top-down and in the round. The neckline features a folded collar for extra warmth, which is followed by a seamless colourwork round yoke that expands in width with regular increases. There is short-row shaping after the ribbing to raise the back of the neck. Once the yoke is complete, you separate for the sleeves to create armholes and then continue with the body. On the body, there is optional short-row shaping to create more room about the chest area to suit your preferences. When you have knitted the body you return to the reserved stitches you separated for the sleeves. The sleeves are knitted top-down and in the round as well.

SIZES

1 (2, 3, 4) 5, 6 [7, 8, 9] 10

HOW TO PICK A SIZE

For a comfortable fit, this jumper should be worn with a positive ease of 5cm/2in to 10cm/4in. Measure the widest section of your chest with a measuring tape. For example, your chest measurement is 90cm/35½in. If you prefer less positive ease, you should pick size 3 for a positive ease of 5cm/2in. If you prefer more positive ease, you should pick size 4 for a positive ease of 15cm/6in.

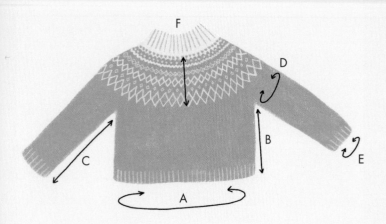

MEASUREMENTS
A: CHEST CIRCUMFERENCE
cm: 76 (86, 95, 105) 115, 125 [135, 145, 155] 165
in: 30 (33¾, 37½, 41¼) 45¼, 49¼ [53¼, 57, 61] 65

B1: SIDE LENGTH – CROPPED
cm: 25 (25.5, 25.5, 25.5) 25.5, 25.5 [25.5, 25.5, 25.5] 25.5
in: 9¾ (10, 10, 10) 10, 10 [10, 10, 10] 10

B2: SIDE LENGTH – REGULAR
cm: 38 (40.5, 43, 45.5) 48.5, 51 [52, 54, 54] 56
in: 15 (16, 17, 18) 19, 20 [20½, 20½, 21] 22

C1: SLEEVE LENGTH – BRACELET
cm: 44.5 (45.5, 45.5, 47) 47, 48 [48, 49.5, 49.5] 49.5
in: 17½ (18, 18, 18½) 18½, 19 [19, 19½, 19½] 19½

C2: SLEEVE LENGTH – FULL
cm: 46.5 (47.5, 48, 50.5) 52.5, 53 [54.5, 54.5, 55.5] 56
in: 18¼ (18¾, 19, 20) 20½, 20¾ [21½, 21½, 21¾] 22

D: UPPER ARM
cm: 29 (30, 32, 35) 39, 41 [42.5, 48, 49] 50
in: 11½ (11¾, 12½, 13¾) 15¼, 16¼ [16¾, 19, 19¼] 19¾

E1: WRIST CIRCUMFERENCE – BRACELET
cm: 18.5 (19, 20.5, 21) 22, 22 [23, 23, 23] 24.5
in: 7¼ (7½, 8, 8¼) 8¾, 8¾ [9, 9, 9] 9¾

E2: WRIST CIRCUMFERENCE – FULL
cm: 20.5 (21, 21.5, 22) 23, 23 [23.5, 23.5, 23.5] 24.5
in: 8 (8¼, 8½, 8¾) 9, 9 [9¼, 9¼, 9¼] 9¾

F: YOKE DEPTH
cm: 23.5 (24, 24.5, 24.5) 25.5, 25.5 [25.5, 26.5, 26.5] 26.5
in: 9¼ (9½, 9¾, 9¾) 10, 10 [10, 10½, 10½] 10½

YARN
Julie Asselin Anatolia (60% kid mohair, 40% silk,
1 ply (lace) weight)
mc – Ale
cc – Naturel

Julie Asselin Nurtured Fine (100% Rambouillet, Targhee
Merino wool mix, DK (light worsted) weight)
mc – Miel
cc – Naturel

Hold one strand of silk mohair in ale and one strand of wool
in miel together to form mc, and one strand of silk mohair in
naturel and one strand of wool in naturel together to form cc.
The yardage is calculated as single strand. You will need the
yardage in each colour.

YARDAGE
METRES – CROPPED
mc: 540 (585, 635, 705) 775, 825 [850, 945, 980] 1020
cc: 120 (130, 143, 160) 176, 186 [199, 215, 229] 239

YARDS – CROPPED
mc: 591 (640, 695, 771) 850, 903 [930, 1034, 1072] 1116
cc: 132 (143, 157, 175) 193, 205 [220, 236, 251] 262

METRES – REGULAR

mc: 660 (730, 815, 940) 1075, 1170 [1275, 1400, 1470] 1600
cc: 120 (130, 143, 160) 176, 186 (199, 215, 229) 239

YARDS – REGULAR

mc: 722 (800, 892, 1028) 1176, 1300 [1400, 1532, 1610] 1750
cc: 132 (143, 157, 175) 193, 204 [218, 236, 251] 262

GAUGE

22 sts x 25 rnds = 10cm/4in in colourwork sts and stockinette st

NEEDLES

Size 4.5mm/US7 circular needles or size necessary to obtain gauge. Use fixed circular knitting needles or cables for interchangeable needles in the following lengths:
40cm/16in
60cm/24in
80cm/32in

NOTIONS

Stitch markers
Tapestry needle
Scrap yarn

BEGIN PATTERN – NECK

Using 4.5mm/US7 needles and cc, co 92 (92, 92, 96) 96, 96 [108, 108, 112] 112 sts using the long-tail cast-on method. Join in the rnd and pm to mark bor.

Work *K1, p1* ribbing for approx 10cm/4in.

FOLDED NECK

Fold the collar in half so the wrong sides are touching. Line up the co edge with the live stitches. Pick up 1 st from the co edge and place it on the left needle. Knit the newly picked up st with the next live stitch on the needle. Cont around the neck in this way, picking up 1 st at a time from the co edge and knitting it together with the next live st on the left needle until you reach the end of the round.

NECK SHORT-ROW SHAPING

K 1 rnd.
SR1 (rs): K 45 (46, 46, 48) 48, 48 [54, 54, 56] 56, w&t.
SR2 (ws): P 68 (69, 69, 72) 72, 72 [81, 81, 84] 84, w&t.
SR3 (rs): K 61 (62, 62, 65) 66, 66 [75, 75, 78] 78, w&t.
SR4 (ws): P 54 (55, 55, 58) 60, 60 [69, 69, 72] 72, w&t.
SR5 (rs): K 47 (48, 48, 51) 54, 54 [63, 63, 66] 66, w&t.
SR6 (ws): P 40 (41, 41, 44) 48, 48 [57, 57, 60] 60, w&t.
SR7 (rs): K – (–, –, –) 42, 42 [51, 51, 54] 54, w&t.

SR8 (ws): P – (–, –, –) 36, 36 [45, 45, 48] 48, w&t.
With rs facing, k to marker, picking up wraps and knitting them together with the wrapped sts as you go.
K 1 rnd, picking up remaining wraps as you go.

SET-UP INC RNDS

Before working the chart, knit the following inc rounds to set up the yoke. Refer to the section corresponding with your chosen size. As the width of the work expands while you work on the yoke, switch to longer circular needles (or cables, if you are using interchangeable needles) for your comfort.

SIZE 1

Rnd 1: K to end of rnd.
Rnd 2: K6 *K5, m1* to last 6 sts, K6 (16 inc). [108 sts]
Rnd 3: K to end of rnd.
Rnd 4: *K6, m1* to end of rnd (18 inc). [126 sts]

SIZE 2

Rnd 1: K to end of rnd. [92 sts]

SIZE 3

Rnd 1: K to end of rnd.
Rnd 2: *K11, m1* to last 4 sts, k4 (8 sts inc). [100 sts]

SIZE 4

Rnd 1: K to end of rnd.
Rnd 2: *K6, m1* to end of rnd (16 sts inc). [112 sts]

SIZE 5

Rnd 1: K to end of rnd.
Rnd 2: *K6, m1* to end of rnd (16 sts inc). [112 sts]
Rnd 3: K to end of rnd.
Rnd 4: *K9, m1* to last 4 sts, k4 (12 sts inc). [124 sts]

SIZE 6
Rnd 1: K to end of rnd.
Rnd 2: *K5, m1* to last 6 sts, k6 (18 sts inc). [114 sts]
Rnd 3: K to end of rnd.
Rnd 4: *K6, m1* to last 6 sts, k6 (18 sts inc). [132 sts]

SIZE 7
Rnd 1: K to end of rnd.
Rnd 2: *K6, m1* to end of rnd (18 sts inc). [126 sts]
Rnd 3: K to end of rnd.
Rnd 4: *K9, m1* to end of rnd (14 sts inc). [140 sts]

SIZE 8
Rnd 1: K to end of rnd.
Rnd 2: *K6, m1* to last 6 sts, k6 (17 sts inc). [125 sts]
Rnd 3: K to end of rnd.
Rnd 4: *K8, m1* to last 5 sts, k5 (15 sts inc). [140 sts]
Rnd 5: K to end of rnd.
Rnd 6: *K11, m1* to last 8 sts, k8 (12 sts inc). [152 sts]

SIZE 9
Rnd 1: K to end of rnd.
Rnd 2: *K7, m1* to end of rnd (16 sts inc). [128 sts]
Rnd 3: K to end of rnd.
Rnd 4: *K8, m1* to end of rnd (16 sts inc). [144 sts]
Rnd 5: K to end of rnd.
Rnd 6: *K9, m1* to end of rnd (16 sts inc). [160 sts]

SIZE 10
Rnd 1: K to end of rnd.
Rnd 2: *K7, m1* to end of rnd. (16 sts inc) [128 sts]
Rnd 3: K to end of rnd.
Rnd 4: k10, m1, *K6, m1* to last 4 sts, k4 (20 sts inc).
[148 sts]
Rnd 5: K to end of rnd.
Rnd 6: K11, m1, *K7, m1* to last 4 sts, k4 (20 sts inc).
[168 sts]

ALL SIZES: Work the rows of the chart shown opposite, making increases as indicated on the chart in the colours stipulated by the key. Note that rnds 1–4 on the chart are knitted for sizes 2–10 only. Before the increases begin, the chart is based on 4 sts, which grows to 12 sts by the end of the increases. Note that the chart repeats 21 (23, 25, 28) 31, 33 [35, 38, 40] 42 times per round.

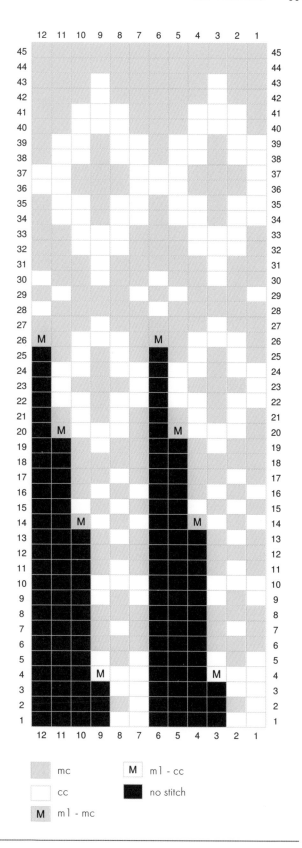

	mc		**M**	m1 - cc
	cc			no stitch
	M m1 - mc			

STITCH COUNT AFTER INCS

After rnd 4, you have (138, 150, 168) 186, 198 [210, 228, 240] 252 sts.

After rnd 14, you have 168 (184, 200, 224) 248, 264 [280, 304, 320] 336 sts.

After rnd 20, you have 210 (230, 250, 280) 310, 330 [350, 380, 400] 420 sts.

After rnd 26, you have 252 (276, 300, 336) 372, 396 [420, 456, 480] 504 sts.

SLEEVE SEPARATION

Using mc, k the first 73 (83, 92, 103) 114, 123 [132, 140, 151] 162 sts for back of body. Transfer the next 53 (55, 58, 65) 72, 75 [78, 88, 89] 90 sts onto scrap yarn for sleeve a. Backwards loop cast-on 11 (11, 12, 13) 14, 15 [16, 18, 19] 20 sts for underarm. Rep across rem sts for front, sleeve b and second underarm. Pm to mark bor. The bor should be on the back of your left shoulder. You have 168 (188, 208, 232) 256, 276 [296, 316, 340] 364 sts on needles.

CHEST SHORT-ROW SHAPING (OPTIONAL)

If you have a bigger chest circumference or prefer a fit with more room around your chest area, knit the following section.

SR1 (rs): K 157 (177, 196, 219) 242, 261 [280, 298, 321] 344, w&t.

SR2 (ws): P 73 (83, 92, 103) 114, 123 [132, 140, 151] 162, w&t.

SR3 (rs): K 68 (78, 87, 98) 109, 118 [127, 135, 146] 157, w&t.

SR4 (ws): P 63 (73, 82, 93) 104, 113 [122, 130, 141] 152, w&t.

SR5 (rs): K 58 (68, 77, 88) 99, 108 [117, 125, 136] 147, w&t.

SR6 (ws): P 53 (63, 72, 83) 94, 103 [112, 120, 131] 142, w&t.

SR7 (rs): K 48 (58, 67, 78) 89, 98 [107, 115, 126] 137, w&t.

SR8 (ws): P 43 (53, 62, 73) 84, 93 [102, 110, 121] 132, w&t.

SR9 (rs): K – (–, –, 68) 79, 88 [97, 105, 116] 127, w&t.

SR10 (ws): P – (–, –, 63) 74, 83 [92, 100, 111] 122, w&t.

SR11 (rs): K – (–, –, –) –, – [–, 95, 106] 117, w&t.

SR12 (ws): P – (–, –, –) –, – [–, 90, 101] 112, w&t.

With rs facing, k to marker, picking up wraps and knitting them together with the wrapped sts as you go.

K 1 rnd, picking up remaining wraps.

BODY

There are two options for body length – cropped or regular. If you are shorter or prefer a cropped jumper, knit the section below labelled "cropped body". If you are taller or prefer a longer jumper, knit the section below labelled "regular body".

CROPPED BODY

Cont working in the rnd in st st until work measures 21 (21.5, 21.1, 21.5) 21.5, 21.5 [21.5, 21.5, 21.5] 21.5cm/8¼ (8½, 8½, 8½) 8½, 8½, [8½, 8½, 8½] 8½in from underarm.

REGULAR BODY

Cont working in the rnd in st st until work measures 34 (36.5, 39, 41.5) 44.5, 47 [48, 50, 50] 52cm/ 13½ (14½, 15½, 16¼) 17½, 18½ [19, 19¾, 19¾] 20½in from underarm.

HEM

Work *K1, p1* ribbing for approx 4cm/1½in. Bind off loosely.

SLEEVE

Transfer held stitches from scrap yarn onto working needle, using mc, pick up an additional 11 (11, 12, 13) 14, 15 [16, 18, 19] 20 sts from underarm. Using mc, k the next 59 (61, 64, 72) 79, 83 [86, 97, 99] 100 sts, pm to mark bor. You have a total of 64 (66, 70, 78) 86, 90 [94, 106, 108] 110 sts.

SLEEVE LENGTHS

There are two sleeve length options – a shorter version (bracelet) and a longer version (full). Cont to your preferred length section.

SHORTER SLEEVE – BRACELET

Rnd 1: Using mc, k to end of rnd.

Dec rnd: *K1, ssk, k to last 3 sts, k2tog, k1* (2 sts dec). Work dec rnd every 7 (8, 8, 6) 5, 4 [4, 3, 3] 3 rnds for a total of 9 (9, 11, 15) 18, 20 [21, 27, 28] 27 times. After final dec, you have 46 (48, 48, 48) 50, 50 [52, 52, 52] 56 sts.

Cont in st st until sleeve measures 40.5 (41.5, 41.5, 43) 43, 44 [44, 45.5, 45.5] 45.5cm/16 (16¼, 16¼, 17) 17, 17¼ [17¼, 18, 18] 18in from underarm. Cont to cuff section.

LONGER SLEEVE – FULL

Rnd 1: Using mc, k to end of rnd.
Dec rnd: *K1, SSK, k to last 3 sts, k2tog, k1*(2 sts dec).

Work dec rnd every 11 (10, 9, 7) 6, 5 [5, 4, 4] 4 rnds a total of 9 (10, 11, 15) 18, 20 [21, 27, 28] 28 times. After final dec, you have 46 (46, 48, 48) 50, 50 [52, 52, 52] 54 sts.

Cont in st st until sleeve measures 42.5 (43.5, 44, 46.5) 48.5, 49 [50.5, 50.5, 51.5] 52cm/16¾ (17¼, 17½, 18½) 19, 19¼ [20, 20, 20¼] 20½in from underarm. Cont to cuff section.

CUFF

Work *K1, p1* ribbing for approx 4cm/1½in. Bind off loosely.

FINISHING

Weave in all ends. Steam or wet block to measurements.

PINGO MITTENS

NOTES

The colourwork chart is read from bottom to top and right to left. These mittens are designed as a mismatched pair, as shown here, with colours A and B reversed. For the second mitten, you simply knit colour A as colour B and vice versa. If you prefer, you can modify the pattern to knit two identical mittens by simply not reversing the colours as instructed in the pattern for mitten two. Please swatch to ensure you have the right gauge before beginning. Stranded colourwork might affect your usual gauge so remember to adjust the needle size as needed.

CONSTRUCTION

These mitts are knitted from bottom-up and in the round. The pair features a colourwork motif throughout. The thumb is a gussetless thumb and uses the afterthought thumb technique. The final mitten top stitches are grafted together using kitchener stitch.

SIZES

S (M) L

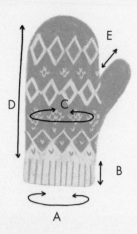

MEASUREMENTS
A: CUFF CIRCUMFERENCE
cm: 16.5 (18) 19
in: 6½ (7) 7½

B: CUFF LENGTH
cm: 4 (5) 5
in: 1½ (2) 2

C: HAND CIRCUMFERENCE
cm: 18 (19) 20
in: 7 (7½) 8

D: HAND LENGTH
cm: 15 (16.5) 18
in: 6 (6½) 7

E: THUMB LENGTH
cm: 3 (4) 4.5
in: 1¼ (1½) 1¾

YARN
Julie Asselin Anatolia (60% kid mohair, 40% silk, 1 ply (lace) weight)
Colour A – Naturel
Colour B – Ale

Julie Asselin Nurtured Fine (100% Rambouillet, Targhee, Merino wool mix, 1 ply (lace) weight)
Colour A – Naturel
Colour B – Miel

Hold one strand of silk mohair in ale and one strand of wool in miel together to form mc, and one strand of silk mohair in naturel and one strand of wool in naturel together to form cc. The yardage is calculated as single strand. You will need the yardage in each colour.

YARDAGE
Calculated based on mismatched pair

COLOUR A
Metres: 50 (65) 80
Yards: 55 (71) 88

COLOUR B
Metres: 50 (65) 80
Yards: 55 (71) 88

GAUGE
24 sts x 26 rnds = 10cm/4in in colourwork sts

NEEDLES
3.25mm/US3 and 3.5mm/US4 needles or sizes necessary to obtain gauge. Use either DPNs, two 60cm/24in circular needles or one longer circular knitting needle for the magic loop method.

NOTIONS
Stitch markers
Scrap yarn
Tapestry needle

BEGIN PATTERN – LEFT MITT/CUFF

Using your choice of stretchy co method, the smaller needles and colour B, co 48 (54) 66 sts. If working with DPNs, divide sts equally across needles. If using the magic loop technique or two circular needles, place half of sts on each needle. Join in the rnd, taking care not to twist sts. Pm to mark bor. Work *k2, p1* ribbing until cuff measures 4 (5) 5cm/1½ (2) 2in from co edge.

HAND

Switch to larger needles. Work the rows of the chart shown opposite. Note that the chart repeats 8 (9) 11 times per round. Rep rnds 1–40 until work measures 7 (8) 9cm/2¾ (3¼) 3½in from co edge.

THUMB HOLE

With colour A, k1. Using scrap yarn, k the next 7 (8) 9 sts, then sl scrap yarn sts back to LH needle.

HAND – CONT'D

Work across the scrap yarn sts following the chart, then cont working the rows of the chart until work is 1cm/¼in shorter than the tip of your middle finger.

MITT DECS

Mitt decs are worked in colour A. Count half the stitches and place unique marker.
Dec rnd: *K1, ssk, knit to 3 sts before marker, k2tog, k1* to end of rnd (4 sts dec).
Rep dec rnd a total of 7 (8) 10 times. You have 20 (22) 26 sts. Cut yarn, leaving a 30cm/12in tail. Graft rem sts together using kitchener stitch.

AFTERTHOUGHT THUMB

The thumb is worked in the rnd using colour A. Remove scrap yarn to prepare for knitting the thumb. Place 7 (8) 9 sts on one needle, pick up 1 st at each end. Place the next 7 (8) 9 sts on next needle, pick up 1 st at each end. You have 18 (20) 22 sts. Knit all sts until thumb is approx 1cm/¼in shorter than the tip of your thumb.
Work *k2tog* until 5 (5) 6 sts remain.
Cut yarn, leaving a 30cm/12in tail. Thread end into tapestry needle and draw it through all sts on needles. Pull up tightly and secure.

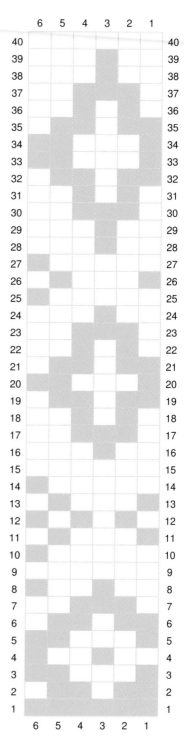

colour A   colour B

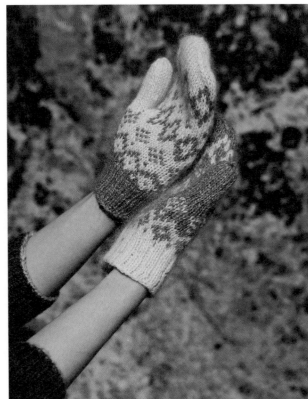

RIGHT MITT

If you want to knit a matching pair, rep all the above steps
for your right mitt. To knit a mismatched pair as shown here,
knit all the colour A sts with colour B and vice versa.

RIGHT MITT THUMB HOLE

With colour B, k 17 (19) 24 sts. Using scrap yarn, k the next
7 (8) 9 sts, then sl scrap yarn sts back to LH needle. Cont
hand section using instructions above.

FINISHING

Weave in all ends. Wet block to measurements.

"WHEN YOU LIVE ON AN ARCTIC ISLAND WHERE
NO ONE IS EVER IN A RUSH, YOU TAKE FOR
GRANTED THE THING EVERYONE ELSE IN THE REST
OF THE UNIVERSE WISHES FOR MORE OF – TIME."

ALPINEPACA JUMPER

While Nunavut isn't home to fluffy sheep and alpacas, it is abundant in wildlife. Polar bears, muskoxen, caribou, Arctic foxes and hares roam the tundra, while narwhal, beluga, walruses and seals glide through the frigid waters of the Arctic Ocean. Due to our remoteness and the lack of road access, we rely on cargo planes to fly our groceries and essentials. In South America, alpacas are often seen transporting goods and are our northern equivalent of cargo planes!

NOTES
This jumper pattern is unisex, has a boxy fit, and comes in ten adult sizes. There are two options for body length options – cropped and regular. Because the jumper is knitted top-down, you can easily customize the length by stopping before or continuing after the recommended body length measurements. There are also two sleeve length options – bracelet length and full length – so you can customize the jumper to fit you best. As each body is unique, please remember that the pattern serves as a guide. Feel free to modify any lengths or to fit your own body and arms. The colourwork chart is read from right to left, bottom to top. The colourwork yoke has long floats, so remember to catch your floats (see page 28). The intended positive ease is about 7.5cm/3in to 13cm/5in. The manchelopi sample is knitted with the yarn held single.

CONSTRUCTION
The jumper is knitted top-down and in the round. The neckline is a high mock neck, which is followed by a seamless colourwork round yoke that expands in width with regular increases. Once the yoke is complete, you separate for the sleeves to create armholes and then continue with the body. There is optional short-row shaping to create more room about the chest area if preferred. When you have knitted the body you return to the reserved stitches you separated for the sleeves. The sleeves are knitted top-down and in the round as well.

SIZES
1 (2, 3, 4) 5, 6 [7, 8, 9] 10

HOW TO PICK A SIZE
For a comfortable fit, this jumper should be worn with a positive ease of 7.5cm/3in to 13cm/5in. Measure the widest section of your chest with a measuring tape. For example, your chest measurement is 100cm/39½in. If you prefer less positive ease, you should pick size 4 for a positive ease of 5cm/2in. If you prefer more positive ease, you should pick size 5 for a positive ease of 18cm/7in.

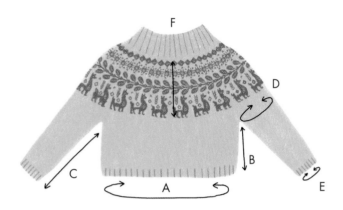

MEASUREMENTS

A: CHEST CIRCUMFERENCE
cm: 79 (89, 98, 105) 118, 130 [137, 150, 158] 168
in: 31 (35, 38½, 41¼) 46½, 51¼ [54, 59, 62¼] 66

B1: SIDE LENGTH – CROPPED
cm: 26.5 (27.5, 27.5, 27.5) 27.5, 27.5 [27.5, 27.5, 27.5] 27.5
in: 10½ (10¾, 10¾, 10¾) 10¾, 10¾ [10¾, 10¾, 10¾] 10¾

B2: SIDE LENGTH – REGULAR
cm: 39.5 (42, 44.5, 47) 49.5, 52 [53.5, 56, 57] 57
in: 15½ (16½, 17½, 18½) 19½, 20½ [21, 22, 22½] 22½

C1: SLEEVE LENGTH – BRACELET
cm: 46 (47, 47, 48.5) 48.5, 49.5 [49.5, 51, 51] 51
in: 18 (18½, 18½, 19) 19, 19½ [19½, 20, 20] 20

C2: SLEEVE LENGTH – FULL
cm: 48 (49, 49.5, 51) 53.5, 54.5 [56, 56, 57] 57.5
in: 19 (19¼, 19½, 20) 21, 21½ [22, 22, 22½] 22¾

D: UPPER ARM
cm: 30 (32, 34, 37) 41, 42 [44, 48, 49] 50
in: 11¾ (12½, 13½, 14½) 16¼, 16½ [17¼, 19, 19¼] 19¾

E: WRIST CIRCUMFERENCE
cm: 23 (23.5, 24, 24.5) 25.5, 25.5 [26, 26, 26] 27
in: 9 (9¼, 9½, 9¾) 10, 10 [10¼, 10¼, 10¼] 10¾

F: YOKE DEPTH
cm: 24 (24, 25, 25) 25.5, 25.5 [25.5, 25.5, 25.5] 25.5
in: 9½ (9½, 9¾, 9¾) 10, 10 [10, 10, 10] 10

YARN
SAMPLE 1
WoolDreamers Manchelopi (100% unspun Manchega wool,
fingering (4 ply) weight)
mc – Blanco
cc – Gris Oscuro

SAMPLE 2
Bare Naked Wools Stone Soup DK (80% Rambouillet,
Lincoln, Columbia and Churro mix; 15% alpaca; 5% tencel,
bamboo and silk mix, DK (light worsted) weight)
mc – Granite
cc – Marble

YARDAGE
METRES – CROPPED
mc: 745 (825, 880, 965) 1075, 1155 [1215, 1330, 1390]
1450
cc: 115 (125, 130, 145) 160, 170 [180, 195, 200] 210

YARDS – CROPPED
mc: 815 (903, 963, 1055) 1176, 1264 [1329, 1455,
1521] 1586
cc: 126 (137, 143, 158) 175, 186 [197, 214, 219] 230

METRES – REGULAR
mc: 860 (975, 1075, 1210) 1380, 1530 [1630, 1830,
1940] 2035
cc: 125 (135, 145, 160) 170, 185 [195, 210, 220] 225

SAMPLE 1

SAMPLE 2

YARDS – REGULAR
mc: 941 (1067, 1176, 1324) 1510, 1674 [1783, 2002, 2122] 2226
cc: 137 (148, 159, 175) 186, 203 [214, 230, 241] 246

GAUGE
22 sts x 22.5 rnds = 10cm/4in in colourwork sts
22 sts x 29 rnds = 10cm/4in in stockinette st

NEEDLES
Size 3.5mm/US4 circular needle or size necessary to obtain gauge. Use fixed circular knitting needles or cables for interchangeable needles in the following lengths:
40cm/16in
60cm/24in
80cm/32in

NOTIONS
Stitch markers
Tapestry needle
Scrap yarn

BEGIN PATTERN – NECK
Using 3.5mm/US4 needles and mc, loosely co 92 (92, 92, 100) 100, 100 [112, 112, 116] 116 sts. Join in the rnd and pm to mark bor.
Work *k1, p1* ribbing until work measures 13cm/5in.

YOKE
Before working the chart, knit the following inc rounds to set up the yoke. Refer to the section correlating with your chosen size. As the width of the work expands while you work on the yoke, switch to longer circular needles (or cables, if you are using interchangeable needles) for your comfort.

SIZE 1
Rnd 1: K to end of rnd.
Rnd 2: *K23, m1* to end of rnd (4 inc). [96 sts]

SIZE 2
Rnd 1: K to end of rnd.
Rnd 2: *K5, m1, k6, m1* to last 4 sts, k4 (16 inc). [108 sts]

SIZE 3
Rnd 1: K to end of rnd.
Rnd 2: *K11, m1* to last 4 sts, k4 (8 inc). [100 sts]
Rnd 3: K to end of rnd.
Rnd 4: *K7, m1* to last 2 sts, k2 (14 inc). [114 sts]

SIZE 4
Rnd 1: K to end of rnd.
Rnd 2: *K8, m1* to last 4 sts, k4 (12 inc). [112 sts]
Rnd 3: K to end of rnd.
Rnd 4: *K8, m1* to end of rnd (14 inc). [126 sts]

SIZE 5
Rnd 1: K to end of rnd.
Rnd 2: *K9, m1* to last sts, k1 (11 inc). [111 sts]
Rnd 3: K to end of rnd.
Rnd 4: *K9, m1* to last 3 sts, k3 (12 inc). [123 sts]
Rnd 5: K to end of rnd.
Rnd 6: *K8, m1* to last 3 sts, k3 (15 inc). [138 sts]

SIZE 6
Rnd 1: K to end of rnd.
Rnd 2: *K12, m1* to last 4 sts, k4 (8 inc). [108 sts]
Rnd 3: K to end of rnd.
Rnd 4: *K5, m1* to last 3 sts, k3 (21 inc). [129 sts]
Rnd 5: K to end of rnd.
Rnd 6: *K6, m1* to last 3 sts, k3 (21 inc). [150 sts]

SIZE 7
Rnd 1: K to end of rnd.
Rnd 2: *K11, m1* to last 2 sts, k2 (10 inc). [122 sts]
Rnd 3: K to end of rnd.
Rnd 4: *K6, m1* to last 2 sts, k2 (20 inc). [142 sts]
Rnd 5: K to end of rnd.
Rnd 6: *K10, m1* to last 2 sts, k2 (14 inc). [156 sts]

SIZE 8
Rnd 1: K to end of rnd.
Rnd 2: *K8, m1* to end of rnd (14 inc). [126 sts]
Rnd 3: K to end of rnd.
Rnd 4: *K5, m1* to last 6 sts, k6 (24 inc). [150 sts]
Rnd 5: K to end of rnd.
Rnd 6: *K6, m1* to last 6 sts, k6 (24 inc). [174 sts]

SIZE 9

Rnd 1: K to end of rnd.
Rnd 2: *K10, m1* to last 6 sts, k6 (11 inc). [127 sts]
Rnd 3: K to end of rnd.
Rnd 4: *K5, m1* to last 2 sts, k2 (25 inc). [152 sts]
Rnd 5: K to end of rnd.
Rnd 6: K11, m1, *k5, m1* to last 6 sts, k6 (28 inc). [180 sts]

SIZE 10

Rnd 1: K to end of rnd.
Rnd 2: *K11, m1* to last 6 sts, k6 (10 inc). [126 sts]
Rnd 3: K to end of rnd.
Rnd 4: *K4, m1* to last 6 sts, k6 (30 inc). [156 sts]
Rnd 5: K to end of rnd.
Rnd 6: *K5, m1* to last 6 sts, k6 (30 inc). [186 sts]

ALL SIZES: Work the rows of the chart shown opposite, making increases as indicated on the chart in the colours stipulated by the key. Before the increases begin, the chart is based on 6 sts, which grows to 16 sts by the end of the increases. Note that the chart repeats 16 (18, 19, 21) 23, 25 [26, 29, 30] 31 times per round.

STITCH COUNT AFTER INCS

After rnd 2, you have 128 (144, 152, 168) 184, 200 [208, 232, 240] 248 sts.
After rnd 6, you have 160 (180, 190, 210) 230, 250 [260, 290, 300] 310 sts.
After rnd 8, you have 192 (216, 228, 252) 276, 300 [312, 348, 360] 372 sts.
After rnd 21, you have 224 (252, 266, 294) 322, 350 [364, 406, 420] 434 sts.
After rnd 36, you have 256 (288, 304, 336) 368, 400 [416, 464, 480] 496 sts.

SLEEVE SEPARATION

Using mc, k the first 74 (85, 92, 100) 112, 124 [131, 144, 152] 160 sts for back of body. Place the next 54 (59, 60, 68) 72, 76 [77, 88, 88] 88 sts onto scrap yarn for sleeve A. Backwards-loop cast-on 12 (11, 14, 14) 16, 16 [17, 18, 20] 22 sts for underarm. Rep over rem sts for front, sleeve B and second underarm. Pm to mark bor. The bor should be on the back of your left shoulder. You have 172 (192, 212, 228) 256, 280 [296, 324, 344] 364 sts on needles.

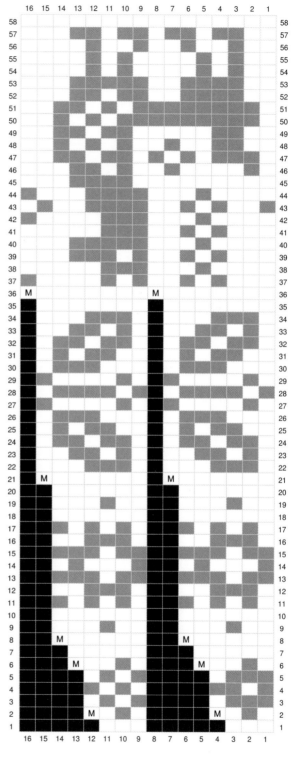

mc | M m1 – mc
cc | no stitch

CHEST SHORT-ROW SHAPING (OPTIONAL)

If you have a bigger chest circumference or prefer a fit with more room around your chest area, knit the following section.

SR1 (rs): K 160 (181, 198, 214) 240, 264 [279, 306, 324] 342, w&t.

SR2 (ws): P 74 (85, 92, 100) 112, 124 [131, 144, 152] 160, w&t.

SR3 (rs): K 69 (80, 87, 95) 107, 119 [126, 139, 147] 155, w&t.

SR4 (ws): P 64 (75, 82, 90) 102, 114 [121, 134, 142] 150, w&t.

SR5 (rs): K 59 (70, 77, 85) 97, 109 [116, 129, 137] 145, w&t.

SR6 (ws): P 54 (65, 72, 80) 92, 104 [111, 124, 132] 140, w&t.

SR7 (rs): K 49 (60, 67, 75) 87, 99 [106, 119, 127] 135, w&t.

SR8 (ws): P 44 (55, 62, 70) 82, 94 [101, 114, 122] 130, w&t.

SR9 (rs): K – (–, –, 65) 77, 89 [96, 109, 117] 125, w&t.

SR10 (ws): P – (–, –, 60) 72, 84 [91, 104, 112] 120, w&t.

SR11 (rs): K – (–, –, –) –, – [–, 99, 107] 115, w&t.

SR12 (ws): P – (–, –, –) –, – [–, 94, 102] 110, w&t.

With rs facing, k to marker, picking up wraps and knitting them together with the wrapped sts as you go.

K 1 round, picking up remaining wraps.

BODY

There are two options for body length – cropped or regular. If you are shorter or prefer a cropped jumper, knit the section below labelled "cropped body". If you are taller or prefer a longer jumper, knit the section below labelled "regular body".

CROPPED BODY

Cont working in the rnd in st st until work measures 21.5 (22, 22, 22) 22, 22 [22, 22, 22] 22cm/8½ (8¾, 8¾, 8¾) 8¾, 8¾ [8¾, 8¾, 8¾] 8¾in from underarm.

REGULAR BODY

Cont working in the rnd in st st until work measures 34.5 (37, 39.5, 42) 45, 47.5 [48.5, 50.5, 52.5] 52.5cm/13½ (14½, 15½, 16½) 17¾, 18¾ [19, 20, 20¾] 20¾in from underarm.

HEM

Work *K1, p1* ribbing until hem measures 5cm/2in. Bind off loosely.

SLEEVE

Transfer held sts from scrap yarn onto working needle, pick up an additional 12 (11, 14, 14) 16, 16 [17, 18, 20] 22 sts from underarm. K the next 60 (65, 67, 75) 80, 84 [86, 97, 98] 99 sts, pm to mark bor. You have a total of 66 (70, 74, 82) 88, 92 [94, 106, 108] 110 sts.

SLEEVE LENGTHS

There are two sleeve length options – a shorter version (bracelet) and a longer version (full). Cont to your preferred length section.

SHORTER SLEEVE – BRACELET

Rnd 1: Using mc, k all sts to end of rnd.

Dec rnd: *K1, ssk, k to last 3 sts, k2tog, k1* (2 sts dec).

Work dec rnd every 7 (7, 7, 6) 5, 4 [4, 3, 3] 3 rnds for a total of 10 [11, 12, 15] 17, 19 [19, 25, 26] 25 times. After final dec, you have 46 (48, 50, 52) 54, 54 [56, 56, 56] 60 sts. Cont in st st until sleeve measures 41 (42, 42, 43.5) 43.5, 44.5 [44.5, 46, 46] 46cm/16¼ (16½, 16½, 17¼) 17¼, 17½ [17½, 18, 18] 18in from underarm. Cont to cuff section.

LONGER SLEEVE – FULL

Rnd 1: Using mc, k to end of rnd.

Dec rnd: *K1, ssk, k to last 3 sts, k2tog, k1* (2 sts dec).

Work dec rnd every 7 (7, 7, 6) 5, 4 [4, 3, 3] 3 rnds for a total of 8 (9, 11, 14) 16, 18 [18, 24, 25] 25 times. After final dec, you have 50 (52, 52, 54) 56, 56 [58, 58, 58] 60 sts. Cont in st st until sleeve measures 43 (44, 44.5, 46) 48.5, 49.5 [51, 51, 52] 52.5cm/17 (17¼, 17½, 18) 19, 19½ [20, 20, 20½] 20¾in from underarm. Cont to cuff section.

CUFF

Work *K1, p1* ribbing until cuff measures 5cm/2in. Bind off loosely.

FINISHING

Weave in all ends. Wet block to measurements.

ALPINEPACA HAT

NOTES

The colourwork chart is read from bottom to top and right to left. Please swatch to ensure you have the right gauge before beginning. Stranded colourwork might affect your usual gauge so please adjust needle size as needed. There are long floats in this design – remember to catch them.

CONSTRUCTION

This hat is knitted from bottom-up and in the round. It features a colourwork motif throughout. The crown is created through decrease intervals. You can choose from folded or single-brim options.

SIZES

1 (2) 3

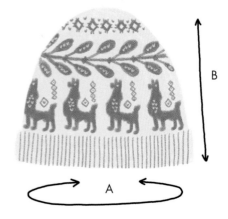

FINISHED MEASUREMENTS
A: HEAD CIRCUMFERENCE
cm: 14 (19) 23
in: 5½ (7½) 9

B: HEIGHT
cm: 21 (21) 21
in: 8¼ (8¼) 8¼

YARN
SAMPLE 1
Bare Naked Wools Stone Soup (80% Rambouillet, Lincoln, Columbia and Churro mix; 15% alpaca, 5% tencel, bamboo and silk mix, DK (light worsted) weight)
mc – Granite
cc – Marble

SAMPLE 2
WoolDreamers Manchelopi (100% unspun Manchega wool, fingering (4 ply) weight)
mc – Blanco
cc – Gris Oscuro

YARDAGE
MC:
Metres: 107 (112) 132
Yards: 117 (123) 145

CC:
Metres: 52 (60) 68
Yards: 57 (66) 75

mc   cc

SAMPLE 1

SAMPLE 2

GAUGE
24 sts x 26 rnds = 10cm/4in in colourwork sts

NEEDLES
3.75mm/US5 circular needles or size necessary to obtain gauge. Use 40cm/16in fixed or interchangeable needles.

NOTIONS
Stitch markers
Tapestry needle

BEGIN PATTERN – BRIM
Using mc, co 96 (112) 128 stitches. Join in the rnd, pm to mark bor.
Work *k2, p2* ribbing until work measures:
Folded brim: 8 (8) 8cm / 3¼ (3¼) 3¼in from co edge.
Fold brim in half. Cut cc.
Single brim: 4 (4) 4cm / 1½ (1½) 1½in from co edge.
Cut cc.

HAT
Work the rows of the chart shown opposite. Note that the chart repeats 6 (7) 8 times per round.

DECS RNDS
Place a marker for every 16th st. You have 6 (7) 8 markers.
Dec rnd: *K1, ssk, k to 3 sts before marker, k2tog, k1* to end of rnd. 12 (14) 16 sts dec.
Rep dec rnd 7 (7) 7 times until you have 12 (14) 16 sts.

Cut yarn, leaving a 30cm/12in tail. Thread end into tapestry needle and draw through all sts on needles. Pull up tightly and secure.

FINISHING
Weave ends in with a tapestry needle. Wet block to measurements.

GLACIAL JUMPER

This jumper is an ode to the alpine glaciers that run through Nunavut Arctic Archipelago. The glaciers we see today were once perfectly formed snowflakes aeons ago. Fun fact: did you know that Nunavut has 14% of the world's glaciers and ice caps?

NOTES

This jumper pattern is unisex, has a boxy fit, and comes in ten adult sizes. There are two options for body length – cropped and regular. Because the jumper is knitted top-down, you can easily customize the length by stopping before or continuing after the recommended body length measurements. There are also two sleeve length options – bracelet length and full length – so you can customize the jumper to fit you best. As each body is unique, please remember that the pattern serves as a guide. Feel free to modify any lengths to fit your own body and arms. The colourwork chart is read from right to left, bottom to top. The colourwork yoke has long floats, so remember to catch your floats (see page 28). The intended positive ease is about 5cm/2in to 10cm/4in. The collar, hem and cuffs are knitted using the corrugated ribbing technique (see page 32) that is less stretchy than normal ribbing. Remember to swatch, check gauge, and size up or down needles as needed.

CONSTRUCTION

This jumper is knitted top-down and in the round. You begin at the neck, which is followed by a seamless colourwork round yoke that expands in width with regular increases. There is optional short-row shaping to raise the back of the neck and also to create more room about the chest area, to suit your preferences. Once the yoke is complete, you separate for the sleeves to create armholes and then continue with the body. When you have knitted the body you return to the reserved stitches you separated for the sleeves. The tapered sleeves are knitted top-down and in the round as well.

SIZES

1 (2, 3, 4) 5, 6 [7, 8, 9] 10

HOW TO PICK A SIZE

For a comfortable fit, this jumper should be worn with a positive ease of 5cm/2in to 10 cm/4in. Measure the widest section of your chest with a measuring tape. For example, your chest measurement is 100cm/39½in. If you prefer less positive ease, you should pick size 4 for a positive ease of 5.5cm/2in. If you prefer more positive ease, you should pick size 5 for a positive ease of 14.5cm/5½in.

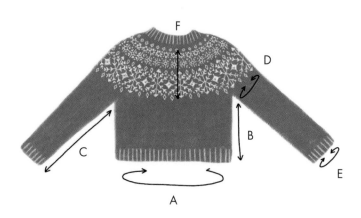

MEASUREMENTS
A: CHEST CIRCUMFERENCE
cm: 74.5 (85.5, 92.5, 105.5) 114.5, 123.5 [134.5, 145.5, 154.5] 163.5
in: 29¼ (33¾, 36½, 41½) 45, 48½ [53, 57¼, 60¾] 64¼

B1: SIDE LENGTH – CROPPED
cm: 20.5 (20.5, 20.5, 20.5) 20.5, 20.5 [20.5, 20.5, 20.5] 20.5
in: 8 (8, 8, 8) 8, 8 [8, 8, 8] 8

B2: SIDE LENGTH – REGULAR
cm: 33 (35.5, 38, 40.5) 43.5, 46 [47, 49, 49] 51
in: 13 (14, 15, 16) 17¼, 18 [18½, 19¼, 19¼] 20

C1: SLEEVE LENGTH – BRACELET
cm: 48.5 (49.5, 49.5, 51) 51, 52 [52, 53.5, 53.5] 53.5
in: 19 (19½, 19½, 20) 20, 20½ [20½, 21, 21] 21

C2: SLEEVE LENGTH – FULL
cm: 50.5 (51.5, 52, 53.5) 56, 57 [58.5, 58.5, 59.5] 60
in: 20 (20¼, 20½, 21) 22, 22½ [23, 23, 23½] 23½

D: UPPER ARM
cm: 29 (30, 32, 35) 39, 41 [44, 48, 49] 50
in: 11½ (11¾, 12½, 13¾) 15¼, 16¼ [17¼, 19, 19¼] 19¾

E: WRIST CIRCUMFERENCE
cm: 20.5 (21, 21, 21.5) 23, 23 [23, 23, 23] 24
in: 8 (8¼, 8¼, 8½) 9, 9 [9, 9, 9] 9½

F: YOKE DEPTH
cm: 21 (21, 21, 21.5) 21.5, 21.5 [21.5, 22.5, 22.5] 22.5
in: 8¼ (8¼, 8¼, 8½) 8½, 8½ [8½, 8¾, 8¾] 8¾

YARN
Cardiff Cashmere Classic (100% Cashmere, DK (light worsted) weight)
mc – 709 Life
cc – 501 Neve

YARDAGE
METRES – CROPPED
mc: 660 (710, 800, 915) 1000, 1090 [1210, 1300, 1375] 1540
cc: 225 (250, 270, 300) 320, 350 [370, 400, 430] 460

YARDS – CROPPED
mc: 722 (777, 875, 1001) 1094, 1200 [1340, 1422, 1504] 1685
cc: 240 (275, 296, 330) 350, 385 [405, 440, 471] 505

METRES – REGULAR
mc: 770 (870, 990, 1120) 1200, 1275 [1375, 1540, 1650] 1790
cc: 260 (300, 350, 400) 430, 460 [500, 530, 560] 590

YARDS – REGULAR
mc: 845 (952, 1085, 1230) 1315, 1400 [1505, 1685, 1805] 1960
cc: 285 (330, 385, 440) 470, 505 [550, 580, 613] 646

GAUGE

22 sts x 30 rnds = 10cm/4in in colourwork sts and stockinette st

NEEDLES

Size 3.5mm/US4 circular needles or size necessary to obtain gauge. Use fixed circular knitting needles or cables for interchangeable needles in the following lengths:
40cm/16in
60cm/24in
80cm/32in

NOTIONS

Stitch markers
Tapestry needle
Scrap yarn

BEGIN PATTERN – NECK

Using 3.5mm/US4 needles and mc, co 84 (84, 84, 88) 96, 96 [100, 100, 100] 104 sts.
Join in the rnd and pm to mark bor.
Begin corrugated ribbing.
Set up rnd: *With mc k1, with cc k1* to end of rnd.
Rnd 1: *With mc k1, with cc p1* to end of rnd.
Rep rnd 1 until corrugated ribbing measures 5cm/2in from co edge.

NECK SHAPING (OPTIONAL)

K 1 rnd.
Begin short-row shaping.
SR1 (rs): K 42 (42, 42, 44) 48, 48 [50, 50, 50] 52, w&t.
SR2 (ws): P 63 (63, 63, 66) 72, 72 [75, 75, 75] 78, w&t.
SR3 (rs): K 58 (58, 58, 61) 67, 67 [70, 70, 70] 73, w&t.
SR4 (ws): P 53 (53, 53, 56) 62, 62 [65, 65, 65] 68, w&t.
SR5 (rs): K 48 (48, 48, 51) 57, 57 [60, 60, 60] 63, w&t.
SR6 (ws): P 43 (43, 43, 46) 52, 52 [55, 55, 55] 58, w&t.
SR7 (rs): K – (–, –, 41) 47, 47 [50, 50, 50] 53, w&t.
SR8 (ws): P – (–, –, 36) 42, 42 [45, 45, 45] 48, w&t.
With rs facing, k to marker, picking up wraps and knitting them together with the wrapped sts as you go.
K 1 rnd, picking up remaining wraps as you go.

YOKE

Before working the chart, knit the following inc rounds to set up the yoke. Refer to the section correlating with your chosen size. As the width of the work expands while you work on the yoke, switch to longer circular needles (or cables, if you are using interchangeable needles) for your comfort.

SIZE 1

Rnd 1: K to end of rnd.
Rnd 2: *K14, m1* end of rnd (6 inc). [90 sts]
Rnd 3: K to end of rnd.
Rnd 4: *K15, m1* to end of rnd (6 inc). [96 sts]

SIZE 2

Rnd 1: K to end of rnd.
Rnd 2: *K8, m1* to last 4 sts, k4 (10 inc). [94 sts]
Rnd 3: K to end of rnd.
Rnd 4: *K9, m1* to last 4 sts, k4 (10 inc). [104 sts]

SIZE 3

Rnd 1: K to end of rnd.
Rnd 2: *K6, m1* to end of rnd (14 inc). [98 sts]
Rnd 3: K to end of rnd.
Rnd 4: *K7, m1* to end of rnd (14 inc). [112 sts]

SIZE 4

Rnd 1: K to end of rnd.
Rnd 2: *K11, m1* to end of rnd (8 inc). [96 sts]
Rnd 3: K to end of rnd.
Rnd 4: *K6, m1* to end of rnd (16 inc). [112 sts]
Rnd 5: K to end of rnd.
Rnd 6: *K7, m1* to end of rnd (16 inc). [128 sts]

SIZE 5

Rnd 1: K to end of rnd.
Rnd 2: *K6, m1* to end of rnd (16 inc). [112 sts]
Rnd 3: K to end of rnd.
Rnd 4: *K7, m1* to end of rnd (16 inc). [128 sts]
Rnd 5: K to end of rnd.
Rnd 6: *K8, m1* to end of rnd (16 inc). [144 sts]

SIZE 6

Rnd 1: K to end of rnd.
Rnd 2: *K6, m1* to end of rnd (16 inc). [112 sts]
Rnd 3: K to end of rnd.
Rnd 4: *K7, m1* to end of rnd (16 inc). [128 sts]
Rnd 5: K to end of rnd.
Rnd 6: K9, m1, *K5, m1* to last 4 sts, k4 (24 inc). [152 sts]

SIZE 7
Rnd 1: K to end of rnd.
Rnd 2: *K5, m1* to end of rnd (20 inc). [120 sts]
Rnd 3: K to end of rnd.
Rnd 4: *K6, m1* to end of rnd (20 inc). [140 sts]
Rnd 5: K to end of rnd.
Rnd 6: *K5, m1* to end of rnd (28 inc). [168 sts]

SIZE 8
Rnd 1: K to end of rnd.
Rnd 2: *K10, m1* to end of rnd (10 inc). [110 sts]
Rnd 3: K to end of rnd.
Rnd 4: *K5, m1* to end of rnd (22 inc). [132 sts]
Rnd 5: K to end of rnd.
Rnd 6: *K6, m1* to end of rnd (22 inc). [154 sts]
Rnd 7: K to end of rnd.
Rnd 8: *K5, m1* to last 4 sts, k4 (30 inc). [184 sts]

SIZE 9
Rnd 1: K to end of rnd.
Rnd 2: *k10, m1* to end of rnd (10 inc). [110 sts]
Rnd 3: K to end of rnd.
Rnd 4: *K5, m1* to end of rnd (22 inc). [132 sts]
Rnd 5: K to end of rnd.
Rnd 6: *K6, m1* to end of rnd (22 inc). [154 sts]
Rnd 7: K to end of rnd.
Rnd 8: *K4, m1* to last 2 sts, k2 (38 inc). [192 sts]

SIZE 10
Rnd 1: K to end of rnd.
Rnd 2: *K10, m1* to last 4 sts, k4 (10 inc). [114 sts]
Rnd 3: K to end of rnd.
Rnd 4: *K4, m1* to last 2 sts, k2 (28 inc). [142 sts]
Rnd 5: K to end of rnd.
Rnd 6: K7, m1, *K4, m1* to last 3 sts, k3 (34 inc). [176 sts]
Rnd 7: K to end of rnd.
Rnd 8: K11, m1, *K7, m1* to last 4 sts, k4 (24 inc). [200 sts]

ALL SIZES: Work the rows of the chart shown below, making increases as indicated on the chart in the colours stipulated by the key. Before the increases begin, the chart is based on 8 sts, which grows to 20 sts by the end of the increases. Note that the chart repeats 12 (13, 14, 16) 18, 19 [21, 23, 24] 25 times per round.

STITCH COUNT AFTER INCS

After rnd 4, you have 144 (156, 168, 192) 216, 228 [252, 276, 288] 300 sts.
After rnd 12, you have 192 (208, 224, 256) 288, 304 [336, 368, 384] 400 sts.
After rnd 23, you have 240 (260, 280, 320) 360, 380 [420, 460, 480] 500 sts.

SLEEVE SEPARATION

Using mc, k the first 69 (80, 86, 100) 110, 118 [132, 142, 151] 160 sts for back of body. Place the next 51 (50, 54, 60) 70, 72 [78, 88, 89] 90 sts on scrap yarn for sleeve A. Backwards-loop cast-on 13 (14, 16, 16) 16, 18 [16, 18, 19] 20 sts for underarm. Rep for front, sleeve B and second underarm over rem sts. Pm to mark bor. The bor is positioned at the back left shoulder of the work. You have 164 (188, 204, 232) 252, 272 [296, 320, 340] 360 sts on needles.

CHEST SHORT-ROW SHAPING (OPTIONAL)

If you have a bigger chest circumference or prefer a fit with more room around your chest area, knit the following section.
SR1 (rs): K 151 (174, 188, 216) 236, 254 [280, 302, 321] 340, w&t.
R2 (ws): P 69 (80, 86, 100) 110, 118 [132, 142, 151] 160, w&t.
SR3 (rs): K 64 (75, 81, 95) 105, 113 [127, 137, 146] 155, w&t.
SR4 (ws): P 59 (70, 76, 90) 100, 108 [122, 132, 141] 150, w&t.
SR5 (rs): K 54 (65, 71, 85) 95, 103 [117, 127, 136] 145, w&t.
SR6 (ws): P 49 (60, 66, 80) 90, 98 [112, 122, 131] 140, w&t.
SR7 (rs): K 44 (55, 61, 75) 85, 93 [107, 117, 126] 135, w&t.
SR8 (ws): P 39 (50, 56, 70) 80, 88 [102, 112, 121] 130, w&t.
SR9 (rs): K – (–, –, 65) 75, 83 [97, 107, 116] 125, w&t.
SR10 (ws): P – (–, –, 60) 70, 78 [92, 102, 111] 120, w&t.
SR11 (rs): K – (–, –, –) –, – [–, 97, 106] 115, w&t.
SR12 (ws): P – (–, –, –) –, – [–, 92, 101] 110, w&t.
With rs facing, k to marker, picking up wraps and knitting them together with the wrapped sts as you go.
K 1 rnd, picking up remaining wraps.

▨ mc	Ⓜ m1 - mc
☐ cc	◼ no stitch

BODY

There are two options for body length – cropped or regular. If you are shorter or prefer a cropped jumper, knit the section following labelled "cropped body". If you are taller or prefer a longer jumper, knit the section following labelled "regular body".

CROPPED BODY

Cont working in the rnd in st st until work measures 15.5 (15.5, 15.5, 15.5) 15.5, 15.5 [15.5, 15.5, 15.5] 15.5cm/6 (6, 6, 6) 6, 6 [6, 6, 6] 6in from underarm.

REGULAR BODY

Cont working in the rnd in st st until work measures 28 (30.5, 33, 35.5) 38.5, 41 [42, 44, 44] 46cm/11 (12, 13, 14) 15¼, 16¼ [16½, 17¼, 17¼] 18in from underarm.

HEM

Begin corrugated ribbing.
Set up rnd: *With mc k1, with cc k1* to end of rnd.
Rnd 1: *With mc k1, with cc, p1* to end of rnd.
Rep rnd 1 until hem measures 5cm/2in. Bind off loosely with mc.

SLEEVE

Transfer held sts from scrap yarn onto working needle, pick up an additional 13 (14, 16, 16) 16, 18 [16, 18, 19] 20 sts from underarm. K the next 58 (57, 62, 68) 78, 81 [86, 97, 99] 100 sts, pm to mark bor. You have a total of 64 (64, 70, 76) 86, 90 [94, 106, 108] 110 sts.

SLEEVE LENGTHS

There are two sleeve length options – a shorter version (bracelet) and a longer version (full). Cont to your preferred length section.

SHORTER SLEEVE – BRACELET

Rnd 1: Using mc, k all sts to end of rnd.

Dec rnd: *K1, ssk, k to last 3 sts, k2tog, k1* (2 sts dec).

Work the dec rnd every 10 (14, 10, 8) 7, 6 [5, 4, 4] 4 rnds for a total of 10 (8, 11, 14) 17, 19 [21, 27, 28] 29 times. After final dec, you have 44 (48, 48, 48) 52, 52 [52, 52, 52] 52 sts.

Cont in st st until sleeve measures 43.5 (44.5, 44.5, 46) 46, 47 [47, 48.5, 48.5] 48.5cm/17¼ (17½, 17½, 18) 18, 18½ [18½, 19, 19] 19in from underarm. Cont to cuff section.

LONGER SLEEVE – FULL

Rnd 1: Using mc, k all sts to end of rnd.

Dec rnd: *K1, ssk, k to last 3 sts, k2tog, k1* (2 sts dec). Work the dec rnd every 11 (14, 10, 8) 7, 7 [6, 5, 5] 5 rnds for a total of 10 (8, 11, 14) 17, 19 [21, 27, 28] 29 times. After final dec, you have 44 (48, 48, 48) 52, 52 [52, 52, 52] 52 sts.

Cont in st st until sleeve measures 45.5 (46.5, 47, 48.5) 51, 52 [53.5, 53.5, 54.5] 55cm/18 (18¼, 18½, 19) 20, 20½ [21, 21, 21½] 21¾in from underarm. Cont to cuff section.

CUFF

Begin corrugated ribbing.
Set up rnd: *With mc k1, with cc k1* to end of rnd.
Rnd 1: *With mc k1, with cc p1* to end of rnd.
Rep rnd 1 until cuff measures 5cm/2in. Bind off loosely with mc.

FINISHING

Weave in all ends. Steam or wet block to measurements.

ARKTOS SOCKS

Derived from the ancient Greek mythology, arktos is the origin for the English word, Arctic. Arktos refers to the northernmost polar region, a place where this design was created.

CHOOSING A SIZE

Socks must be worn with a little negative ease for a comfortable and secure fit. The pattern provides 11 sizes, so measure your foot circumference and length, then use the following notes on the required negative ease to select the best size for you.

FOOT CIRCUMFERENCE: For children, the finished sock foot circumference should be approximately 1.3cm/½in less than the circumference of the actual foot. For adults, the finished sock foot circumference should be approximately 2.5cm/1in less than the circumference of the actual foot. So, if making socks for a child with a foot circumference of 15cm/6in, the circumference of the sock foot should be approximately 14cm/5½in. If making socks for an adult with a foot circumference of 30.5cm/12in, the circumference of the sock foot should be approximately 28cm/11in.

FOOT LENGTH: For children, the length of the finished sock foot should be approximately 6mm/¼in less than the length of the actual foot. For adults, the length of the finished sock foot should be approximately 1.3cm/½in less than the length of the actual foot.

IDENTIFYING THE CORRECT SIZE: When choosing a size, measure the foot circumference, work out the desired measurement of the finished sock with the correct negative ease, then select the size matching this measurement. If the length of the finished sock foot isn't right, you can simply knit a greater or lesser number of rounds than stated in the pattern to make the foot length as long or as short as you need it to be.

SOCK LENGTH: When it comes to the length of the sock from the ankle upwards, the lengths in the pattern are just a guideline. Feel free to adjust the sock height according to your own preference.

CONSTRUCTION

The socks are knitted from top-down and in the round. The pair features a colourwork motif throughout. The heels are knitted using the afterthought heel technique. The final heel and toe stitches are grafted together using kitchener stitch.

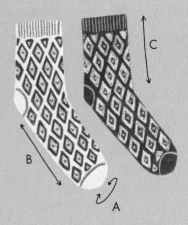

NOTES

The colourwork chart is read from bottom to top and right to left. These socks are designed as a mismatched pair, as shown here, with the colours reversed. For the second sock, you simply knit colour A as colour B and vice versa. If you prefer, you can modify the pattern to knit two identical socks by simply not reversing the colours as instructed in the pattern for sock two. Please swatch to ensure you have the right gauge before beginning. Stranded colourwork might affect your usual gauge so remember to adjust the needle size as needed.

SIZES

1, 2, 3, (4, 5, 6) 7, 8, 9 [10, 11]

MEASUREMENTS

A: FOOT CIRCUMFERENCE

measured across the widest part of the foot
cm: 11.5, 14, 15.25 (16.5, 17.75, 20.25) 23, 25.5, 28 [30.5, 31.75]
in: 4½, 5½, 6 (6½, 7, 8) 9, 10, 11 [12, 12½]

B: FOOT LENGTH

measured from heel to toe
cm: 12, 14, 17 (19, 21, 24) 26, 28, 32 [33, 33]
in: 4¾, 5½, 6¾ (7½, 8¼, 9½) 10¼, 11, 12½ [13, 13]

C: SOCK HEIGHT

measured from heel to co edge
cm: 8.25, 8.25, 8.25 (11.5, 11.5, 14) 14, 14, 14, [14, 14]
in: 3¼, 3¼, 3¼ (4½, 4½, 5½) 5½, 5½, 5½ [5½, 5½]

YARN

Big Little Yarn Co Trusty Sock Base (75% superwash Merino. 25% nylon, 5 ply (sport) weight)
Colour A – Kuri
Colour B – Washi

YARDAGE

Calculated based on a mismatched pair

COLOUR A

Metres: 56, 84, 111 (140, 167, 195) 223, 278, 306 [334, 362]
Yards: 62, 92, 122 (154, 183, 214) 244, 305, 335 [366, 396]

COLOUR B

Metres: 56, 84, 111 (140, 167, 195) 223, 278, 306 [334, 362]
Yards: 62, 92, 122 (154, 183, 214) 244, 305, 335 [366, 396]

GAUGE

33 sts x 40 rnds = 10cm/4in in colourwork sts

NEEDLES

Size 2.25mm/US1 needles or size necessary to obtain gauge. Use either DPNs, two 60cm/24in circular knitting needles or one longer circular needle for the magic loop method.

NOTIONS
Stitch markers
Scrap yarn
Tapestry needle

BEGIN PATTERN – FIRST SOCK/CUFF
Using your choice of stretchy co method and colour B, co 40, 48, 48 (56, 56, 64) 72, 80, 88 [96, 104] sts. If working with four or five DPNs, divide sts equally across three or four needles. If using the magic loop method or two circular needles, place half the sts on each needle. Join in the rnd, taking care not to twist sts. Pm to mark bor. Work *K1, p1* ribbing until cuff measures 2.5cm/1in from co edge.
K 1 rnd.

LEG
Work the rows of the chart shown below. Note that the chart repeats 5, 6, 6 (7, 7, 8) 9, 10, 11 [12, 13] times per round. Rep rounds 1–16 until work measures 8.25, 8.25, 8.25 (11.5, 11.5, 14) 14, 14, 14, [14, 14]cm/3¼, 3¼, 3¼ (4½, 4½, 5½) 5½, 5½, 5½ [5½, 5½]in from co edge.

colour A   colour B

HEEL OPENING – AFTERTHOUGHT HEEL SET UP
Using scrap yarn, k the first 20, 24, 24 (28, 28, 32) 36, 40, 44 [48, 52] sts, then sl scrap yarn sts back onto LH needle.

FOOT
Work across the scrap yarn sts following the chart, then cont working the rows of the chart until work measures 5, 5.75, 8.25 (9, 10.75, 12.75) 14, 16, 17.75 [19, 19]cm/2, 2¼, 3¼ (3½, 4¼, 5) 5½, 6¼, 7 [7½, 7½]in from heel opening or 7, 8.25, 9.5 (10.25, 10.25, 11.5) 12, 12, 14 [14, 14]cm/2¾, 3¼, 3¾ (4, 4, 4½) 4¾, 4¾, 5½ [5½, 5½]in shorter than desired foot length.

TOE SHAPING
The toe is worked in the rnd in colour B. Count half your sts and place an additional marker.
Rnd 1: *Ssk, k to 2 sts before marker, k2tog* rep to end of rnd (4 dec).
Rnd 2: K to end of rnd.
Rep rnds 1 and 2 a total of 5, 6, 6 (7, 7, 8) 8, 8, 8 [8, 8] times. You have 20, 24, 24 (28, 28, 32) 40, 48, 56 [64, 72] sts.
Rep rnd 1 a total of 3, 4, 4 (5, 5, 5) 6, 8, 9 [9, 9] times. You have 8, 8, 8 (8, 8, 12) 16, 16, 20 [28, 36] sts.
Cut yarn, leaving a 30cm/12in tail. Graft rem sts together using kitchener stitch.

AFTERTHOUGHT HEEL
The heel is worked in the rnd using colour B.
Remove scrap yarn to prepare for knitting the heel. Place 20, 24, 24 (28, 28, 32) 36, 40, 44 [48, 52] leg sts on one needle, pick up 1 st at each end. Place 20, 24, 24 (28, 28, 32) 36, 40, 44 [48, 52] foot sts on one needle, pick up 1 st at each end. You have 22, 26, 26 (30, 30, 34) 38, 42, 46 [50, 54] sts on each needle for a total of 44, 52, 52 (60, 60, 68) 76, 84, 92 [100, 108] sts.

SET-UP RND
Pm at beginning of first needle to mark bor. Attach colour B, leaving a tail of at least 15cm/6in.
Rnd 1: K 22, 26, 26 (30, 30, 34) 38, 42, 46 [50, 54] sts, pm, k to end of rnd. Note: If desired, twist picked up "corner" sts to eliminate holes.
Rnd 2: K to end of rnd.

HEEL DECS

Rnd 1: *Ssk, k to 2 sts before marker, k2tog* rep to end of rnd (4 dec).

Rnd 2: K to end of rnd.

Rep rnds 1 and 2 a total of 6, 7, 7 (8, 8, 9) 10, 11, 12 [12, 12] times. You have 20, 24, 24 (28, 28, 32) 36, 40, 44 [52, 60] sts.

Rep rnd 1 a total of 2, 3, 3 (4, 4, 4) 5, 5, 6 [8, 8] times. You have 12, 12, 12 (12, 12, 16) 16, 20, 20 [20, 28] sts.

Cut yarn, leaving a tail of 30cm/12in. Graft rem sts together using kitchener stitch.

SECOND SOCK

If you want to knit a matching pair, rep the above steps for your second sock. To knit a mismatched pair as shown here, reverse the colours, knitting colour A as colour B and vice versa.

FINISHING

Weave in all ends. Wet block socks to measurements.

ARKTOS MITTENS

NOTES
The colourwork chart is read from bottom to top and right to left. These mittens are designed as a mismatched pair, as shown here, with colours A and B reversed. For the second mitten, you simply knit colour A as colour B and vice versa. If you prefer, you can modify the pattern to knit two identical mittens by simply not reversing the colours as instructed in the pattern for mitten two. Please swatch to ensure you have the right gauge before beginning. Stranded colourwork might affect your usual gauge so remember to adjust the needle size as needed.

CONSTRUCTION
These mitts are knitted from bottom-up and in the round. The pair features colourwork motif throughout. The thumb is a gussetless thumb and uses the afterthought thumb technique. The final mitten top stitches are grafted together using kitchener stitch.

SIZES
S (M) L

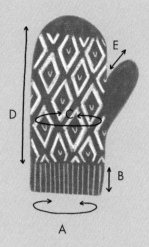

MEASUREMENTS
A: CUFF CIRCUMFERENCE
cm: 16.5 (18) 19
in: 6½ (7) 7½

B: CUFF LENGTH
cm: 4 (5) 5
in: 1½ (2) 2

C: HAND CIRCUMFERENCE
cm: 18 (19) 20
in: 7 (7½) 8

D: HAND LENGTH
cm: 15 (16.5) 18
in: 6 (6½) 7

E: THUMB LENGTH
cm: 3 (4) 4.5
in: 1¼ (1½) 1¾

YARN
WoolDreamers Mota (100% Merino Entrefina and
Manchega Wool, DK (light worsted) weight)
Colour A – 840
Colour B – Blanco Naturel

YARDAGE
Calculated based on mismatched pair

COLOUR A
Metres: 50 (65) 80
Yards: 55 (71) 88

COLOUR B
Metres: 50 (65) 80
Yards: 55 (71) 88

GAUGE
24 sts x 26 rnds = 10cm/4in in colourwork sts

NEEDLES
3.25mm/US3 and 3.5mm/US4) needles or sizes
necessary to obtain gauge. Use either DPNs, two circular
needles or one circular needles for magic loop method.

NOTIONS
Stitch markers
Scrap yarn
Tapestry needle

BEGIN PATTERN – LEFT MITT/CUFF

Using your choice of stretchy co method, the smaller needles and colour B, co 48 (56) 64 sts. If working with DPNs, divide sts equally across needles. If using the magic loop method or two circular needles, place half the sts on each needle. Join in the rnd, taking care not to twist sts. Pm to mark bor. Work *k2, p2* ribbing until cuff measures 4 (5) 5cm/1½ (2) 2in from co edge.

HAND

Switch to larger needles. Work the rows of the chart shown below. Note that the chart repeats 6 (7) 8 times per round. Rep rnds 1–16 until work measures 7 (8) 9cm/2¾ (3¼) 3½in from co edge.

colour A   colour B

THUMB HOLE

With colour B, k1. Using scrap yarn, k the first 7 (8) 9 sts, then sl scrap yarn sts back to LH needle.

HAND – CONT'D

Work across the scrap yarn sts following the chart, then cont working the rows of the chart until work is 1cm/¼in shorter than the tip of your middle finger.

MITT DECS

Mitt decs are worked in colour B. Count half the stitches and place unique marker.
Dec rnd: *K1, ssk, knit to 3 sts before marker, k2tog, k1* to end of rnd (4 sts dec).
Rep dec rnd a total of 7 (8) 9 times. You have 20 (24) 28 sts.
Cut yarn, leaving a 30cm/12in tail. Graft rem sts together using kitchener stitch.

AFTERTHOUGHT THUMB

The thumb is worked in the rnd using colour A. Remove scrap yarn to prepare for knitting the thumb. Place 7 (8) 9 sts on one needle, pick up 1 st at each end. Place the next 7 (8) 9 sts on next needle, pick up 1 st at each end. You have 18 (20) 22 sts. Knit all sts until thumb is approx 1cm/¼in shorter than the tip of your thumb. Work *k2tog* until 5 (5) 6 sts remain. Cut yarn, leaving a 30cm/12in tail. Thread end into tapestry needle and draw it through all sts on needles. Pull up tightly and secure.

RIGHT MITT

If you want to knit a matching pair, rep all the above steps for your right mitt.
To knit a mismatched pair as shown here, knit all the colour A sts with colour B and vice versa.

RIGHT MITT THUMB HOLE

With colour A, k 17 (20) 23 sts. Using scrap yarn, k the next 7 (8) 9 sts, then sl scrap yarn sts back to LH needle. Cont hand section using instructions above.

FINISHING

Weave in all ends. Wet block to measurements.

"THERE IS SOMETHING SO SATISFYING ABOUT MAKING YOUR OWN GARMENTS ONE STITCH AT A TIME. IT IS SLOW, INTENTIONAL, AND PURPOSEFUL."

DORSET SOCKS

Dorset mimics the colours, shapes and forms of the art and tools of the prehistoric culture that thrived in the Canadian Arctic during 1AD.

CHOOSING A SIZE

Socks must be worn with a little negative ease for a comfortable and secure fit. The pattern provides 11 sizes, so measure your foot circumference and length, then use the following notes on the required negative ease to select the best size for you.

FOOT CIRCUMFERENCE: For children, the finished sock foot circumference should be approximately 1.3cm/½in less than the circumference of the actual foot. For adults, the finished sock foot circumference should be approximately 2.5cm/1in less than the circumference of the actual foot. So, if making socks for a child with a foot circumference of 15cm/6in, the circumference of the sock foot should be approximately 14cm/5½in. If making socks for an adult with a foot circumference of 30.5cm/12in, the circumference of the sock foot should be approximately 28cm/11in.

FOOT LENGTH: For children, the length of the finished sock foot should be approximately 6mm/¼in less than the length of the actual foot. For adults, the length of the finished sock foot should be approximately 1.3cm/½in less than the length of the actual foot.

IDENTIFYING THE CORRECT SIZE: When choosing a size, measure the foot circumference, work out the desired measurement of the finished sock with the correct negative ease, then select the size matching this measurement. If the length of the finished sock foot isn't right, you can simply knit a greater or lesser number of rounds than stated in the pattern to make the foot length as long or as short as you need it to be.

SOCK LENGTH: When it comes to the length of the sock from the ankle upwards, the lengths in the pattern are just a guideline. Feel free to adjust the sock height according to your own preference.

CONSTRUCTION

The socks are knitted from top-down and in the round. The pair features a colourwork motif throughout. The heels are knitted using the afterthought heel technique. The final heel and toe stitches are grafted together using kitchener stitch.

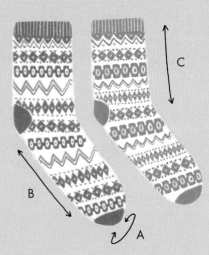

NOTES

The colourwork chart is read from bottom to top and right to left. These socks are designed as a mismatched pair, as shown here, with colours B and C reversed. For the second sock, you simply knit colour B as colour C and vice versa. If you prefer, you can modify the pattern to knit two identical socks by simply not reversing the colours as instructed in the pattern for sock two. Please swatch to ensure you have the right gauge before beginning. Stranded colourwork might affect your usual gauge so remember to adjust the needle size as needed.

SIZES

1, 2, 3, (4, 5, 6) 7, 8, 9 [10, 11]

MEASUREMENTS
A: FOOT CIRCUMFERENCE
measured across the widest part of the foot
cm: 11.5, 14, 15.25 (16.5, 17.75, 20.25) 23, 25.5, 28 [30.5, 31.75]
in: 4½, 5½, 6 (6½, 7, 8) 9, 10, 11 [12, 12½]

B: FOOT LENGTH
measured from heel to toe
cm: 12, 14, 17 (19, 21, 24) 26, 28, 32 [33, 33]
in: 4¾, 5½, 6¾ (7½, 8¼, 9½) 10¼, 11, 12½ [13, 13]

C: SOCK HEIGHT
measured from heel to co edge
cm: 9, 12, 12 (15, 15, 15) 18.5, 18.5, 18.5 [18.5, 18.5]
in: 3½, 4¾, 4¾ (6, 6, 6) 7¼, 7¼, 7¼ [7¼, 7¼]

YARN
Biches & Bûches Le Petit Lambswool (100% lambswool, fingering (4 ply) weight)
Colour A – White
Colour B – Grey Brown
Colour C – Medium Grey

YARDAGE
Calculated based on a mismatched pair

COLOUR A
Metres: 56, 84, 111 (140, 167, 195) 223, 278, 306 [334, 362]
Yards: 62, 92, 122 (154, 183, 214) 244, 305, 335 [366, 396]

COLOUR B
Metres: 28, 42, 56 (70, 84, 95) 111, 140, 153 [167, 181]
Yards: 31, 46, 62 (77, 92, 104) 122, 154, 168 [183, 198]

COLOUR C
Metres: 28, 42, 56 (70, 84, 95) 111, 140, 153 [167, 181]
Yards: 31, 46, 62 (77, 92, 104) 122, 154, 168 [183, 198]

GAUGE
33 sts x 40 rnds = 10cm/4in in colourwork sts

NEEDLES
Size 2.25mm/US1 needles or size necessary to obtain gauge. Use either DPNs, two 60cm/24in circular knitting needles or one longer circular needle for the magic loop method.

NOTIONS
Stitch markers
Scrap yarn
Tapestry needle

BEGIN PATTERN – FIRST SOCK/CUFF
Using your choice of stretchy co method and colour C, co 40, 48, 48 (56, 56, 64) 72, 80, 88 [96, 104] sts. If working with four or five DPNs, divide sts equally across three or four needles. If using the magic loop method or two circular needles, place half the sts on each needle. Join in the rnd, taking care not to twist sts. Pm to mark bor. Work *k2, p2* ribbing until cuff measures 5cm/2in from co edge. K 1 rnd.

LEG
Work the rows of the chart shown opposite. Note that the chart repeats 5, 6, 6 (7, 7, 8) 9, 10, 11 [12, 13] times per round.
Work rnds 1–42 once and then rep rnds 8–42 until work measures 8.25, 8.25, 8.25 (11.5, 11.5, 14) 14, 14, 14, [14, 14]cm/3¼, 3¼, 3¼ (4½, 4½, 5½) 5½, 5½, 5½ [5½, 5½] in from co edge. Note: When you reach the desired length, ensure you end on a plain rnd with colour A (i.e. rnds 16, 26, 33, 42).

HEEL OPENING – AFTERTHOUGHT HEEL SET UP
Using scrap yarn, k the first 20, 24, 24 (28, 28, 32) 36, 40, 44 [48, 52] sts, then sl scrap yarn sts back onto LH needle.

FOOT
Work across the scrap yarn sts following the chart, then cont working rows 8–42 of the chart until work measures 5, 5.75, 8.25 (9, 10.75, 12.75) 14, 16, 17.75 [19, 19]cm/2, 2¼, 3¼ (3½, 4¼, 5) 5½, 6¼, 7 [7½, 7½]in from heel opening or 7, 8.25, 9.5 (10.25, 10.25, 11.5) 12, 12, 14 [14, 14]cm/2¾,

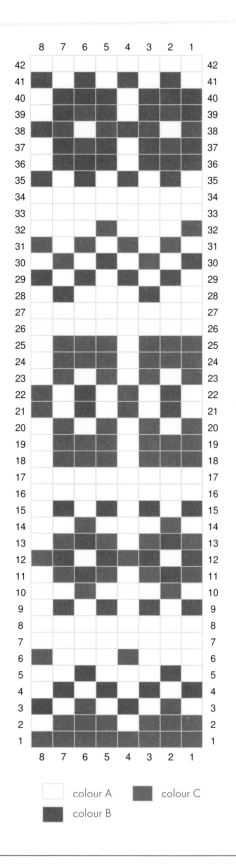

colour A

colour B

colour C

3¼, 3¾ (4, 4, 4½) 4¾, 4¾, 5½ [5½, 5½]in shorter than desired foot length.

Note: When you reach the desired length, ensure you end on a plain rnd with colour A (i.e. rnds 16, 26, 33, 42).

TOE SHAPING

The toe is worked in the rnd in colour C. Count half your sts and place additional marker.

Rnd 1: *Ssk, k to 2 sts before marker, k2tog* rep to end of rnd (4 dec).

Rnd 2: K to end of rnd.

Rep rnds 1 and 2 a total of 5, 6, 6 (7, 7, 8) 8, 8, 8 [8, 8] times. You have 20, 24, 24 (28, 28, 32) 40, 48, 56 [64, 72] sts.

Rep rnd 1 a total of 3, 4, 4 (5, 5, 5) 6, 8, 9 [9, 9] times. You have 8, 8, 8 (8, 8, 12) 16, 16, 20 [28, 36] sts.

Cut yarn, leaving a 30cm/12in tail. Graft sts together using kitchener stitch.

AFTERTHOUGHT HEEL

The heel is worked in the rnd using colour C.

Remove scrap yarn to prepare for knitting the heel. Place 20, 24, 24 (28, 28, 32) 36, 40, 44 [48, 52] leg sts on one needle, pick up 1 st at each end. Place 20, 24, 24 (28, 28, 32) 36, 40, 44 [48, 52] foot sts on one needle, pick up 1 st at each end. You have 22, 26, 26 (30, 30, 34) 38, 42, 46 [50, 54] sts on each needle for a total of 44, 52, 52 (60, 60, 68) 76, 84, 92 [100, 108] sts.

SET-UP RND

Pm at beginning of first needle to mark bor. Attach colour C, leaving a tail of at least 15cm/6in.

Rnd 1: K 22, 26, 26 (30, 30, 34) 38, 42, 46 [50, 54] sts, pm, k to end of rnd. Note: If desired, twist picked up "corner" sts to eliminate holes.

Rnd 2: K to end of rnd.

HEEL DECS

Rnd 1: *Ssk, k to 2 sts before marker, k2tog* rep to end of rnd (4 dec).

Rnd 2: K to end of rnd.

Rep rnds 1 and 2 a total of 6, 7, 7 (8, 8, 9) 10, 11, 12 [12, 12] times. You have 20, 24, 24 (28, 28, 32) 36, 40, 44 [52, 60] sts.

Rep rnd 1 a total of 2, 3, 3 (4, 4, 4) 5, 5, 6 [8, 8] times. You have 12, 12, 12 (12, 12, 16) 16, 20, 20 [20, 28] sts.

Cut yarn, leaving a tail of 30cm/12in. Graft rem together using kitchener stitch.

SECOND SOCK

If you want to knit a matching pair, rep all the above steps for your second sock.

To knit a mismatched pair as shown here, knit all the colour C sts with colour B and vice versa.

FINISHING

Weave in all ends. Wet block socks to measurements.

SNOWDUST HAT

NOTES

The colourwork chart is read from bottom to top and right to left. Please swatch to ensure you have the right gauge before beginning. Stranded colourwork might affect your usual gauge so please adjust needle size as needed.

CONSTRUCTION

This hat is knitted from bottom-up and in the round. It features a colourwork motif throughout. The crown is created by regularly spaced decreases.

SIZES

1 (2) 3

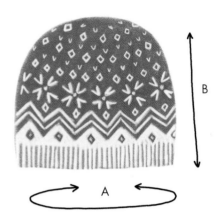

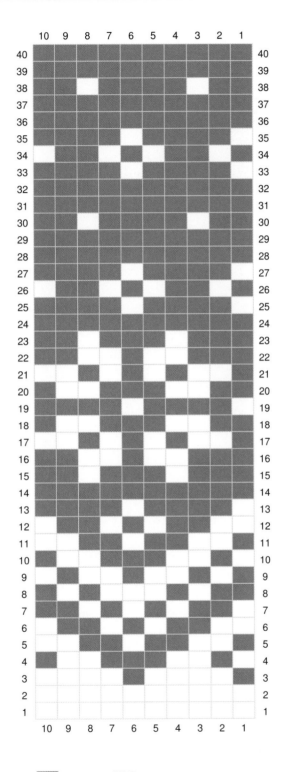

MEASUREMENTS
A: HEAD CIRCUMFERENCE
cm: 14 (19) 23
in: 5½ (7½) 9

B: HEIGHT
cm: 21 (21) 21
in: 8¼ (8¼) 8¼

YARN
Woollentwine Shetland/Romney 4ply (50% Shetland wool,
50% Romney wool, sport (5 ply) weight)
mc – Walnut
cc – Cream

YARDAGE
MC
Metres: 108 (120) 132
Yards: 118 132) 145

CC
Metres: 54 (60) 68
Yards: 60 (66) 75

GAUGE
24 sts x 26 rnds = 10cm/4in in colourwork sts

NEEDLES
3.5mm/US4 circular needles or size necessary to obtain
gauge. Use 40cm/16in fixed or interchangeable needles.

 mc   cc

NOTIONS
Stitch markers
Tapestry needle

BEGIN PATTERN – BRIM
Using cc, co 100 (110) 120 sts. Join in the rnd, taking care not to twist sts. Pm to mark bor. Work *k1, p1* ribbing until brim measures 3.5cm/1½in from co edge.

HAT
Work the rows of the chart shown opposite. Note that the chart repeats 10 (11) 12 times per round.
Work rnds 1–40 once and then rep rnds 25–42 until work measures 19 (19) 19cm/7½ (7½) 7½in from co edge.

DECREASE RNDS
Place a marker for every 10 (11) 12 st. You have 10 (10) 10 markers.
Dec rnd: *K1, ssk, k to 3 sts before marker, k2tog, k1* to end of rnd. 10 (10) 10 sts dec.
Rep dec rnd a total of 9 (10) 11 times until you have 10 (10) 10 sts.

Cut yarn, leaving a 30cm/12in tail. Thread end into tapestry needle and draw through all sts on needles. Pull up tightly and secure.

FINISHING
Weave ends in with a tapestry needle. Wet block to measurements.

SNOWDUST SOCKS

CHOOSING A SIZE

Socks must be worn with a little negative ease for a comfortable and secure fit. The pattern provides 9 sizes, so measure your foot circumference and length, then use the following notes on the required negative ease to select the best size for you.

FOOT CIRCUMFERENCE: For children, the finished sock foot circumference should be approximately 1.3cm/½in less than the circumference of the actual foot. For adults, the finished sock foot circumference should be approximately 2.5cm/1in less than the circumference of the actual foot. So, if making socks for a child with a foot circumference of 15cm/6in, the circumference of the sock foot should be approximately 14cm/5½in. If making socks for an adult with a foot circumference of 30.5cm/12in, the circumference of the sock foot should be approximately 28cm/11in.

FOOT LENGTH: For children, the length of the finished sock foot should be approximately 6mm/¼in less than the length of the actual foot. For adults, the length of the finished sock foot should be approximately 1.3cm/½in less than the length of the actual foot.

IDENTIFYING THE CORRECT SIZE: When choosing a size, measure the foot circumference, work out the desired measurement of the finished sock with the correct negative ease, then select the size matching this measurement. If the length of the finished sock foot isn't right, you can simply knit a greater or lesser number of rounds than stated in the pattern to make the foot length as long or as short as you need it to be.

SOCK LENGTH: When it comes to the length of the sock from the ankle upwards, the lengths in the pattern are just a guideline. Feel free to adjust the sock height according to your own preference.

CONSTRUCTION

The socks are knitted from top-down and in the round. The pair features a colourwork motif throughout. The heels are knitted using the afterthought heel technique. The final heel and toe stitches are grafted together using kitchener stitch.

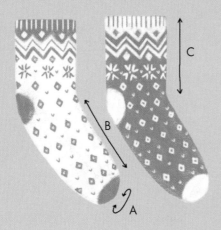

C: SOCK HEIGHT
measured from heel to co edge
cm: 8.25, 8.25, 8.25 (11.5, 11.5) 14, 14, 14, [14]
in: 3¼, 3¼, 3¼ (4½, 4½) 5½, 5½, 5½ [5½]

YARN
Woollentwine Shetland/Romney (50% Shetland wool,
50% Romney wool, 4ply (fingering) weight)
Colour A – Cream
Colour B – Walnut

YARDAGE
Calculated based on a mismatched pair

COLOUR A
Metres: 56, 84, 111 (140, 167) 223, 278, 306 [334]
Yards: 62, 92, 123 (154, 183) 244, 305, 335 [366]

COLOUR B
Metres: 56, 84, 111 (140, 167) 223, 278, 306 [334]
Yards: 62, 92, 123 (154, 183) 244, 305, 335 [366]

GAUGE
33 sts x 40 rows = 10cm/4in in colourwork sts

NEEDLES
Size 2.25mm/US 1 needles or size necessary to obtain
gauge. Use either DPNs, two 60cm/24in circular knitting
needles or one longer circular needle for the magic
loop method.

NOTIONS
Stitch markers
Scrap yarn
Tapestry needle

BEGIN PATTERN – FIRST SOCK/CUFF
Using your choice of stretchy co method and colour B, co
40, 50, 50 (60, 60) 70, 80, 90 [100] sts. If working with four
or five DPNs, divide sts equally across three or four needles.
If using the magic loop method or two circular needles, place
half the sts on each needle. Join in the rnd, taking care not
to twist sts. Pm to mark bor. Work *k1, p1* ribbing until cuff
measures 1.5cm/½in from co edge.

NOTES
The colourwork chart is read from bottom to top and right
to left. These socks are designed as a mismatched pair, as
shown here, with the colours reversed. For the second sock,
you simply knit colour A as colour B and vice versa. If you
prefer, you can modify the pattern to knit two identical socks
by simply not reversing the colours as instructed in the pattern
for sock two. Please swatch to ensure you have the right
gauge before beginning. Stranded colourwork might affect
your usual gauge so remember to adjust the needle size
as needed.

SIZES
1, 2, 3 (4, 5) 6, 7, 8 (9)

MEASUREMENTS
A: FOOT CIRCUMFERENCE
measured across the widest part of the foot
cm: 11.5, 14, 15.25 (16.5, 17.75) 23, 25.5, 28 [31.75]
in: 4½, 5½, 6 (6½, 7) 9, 10, 11 [12½]

B: FOOT LENGTH
measured from heel to toe
cm: 12, 14, 17 (19, 21) 26, 28, 32 [33]
in: 4¾, 5½, 6¾ (7½, 8¼) 10¼, 11, 12½ [13]

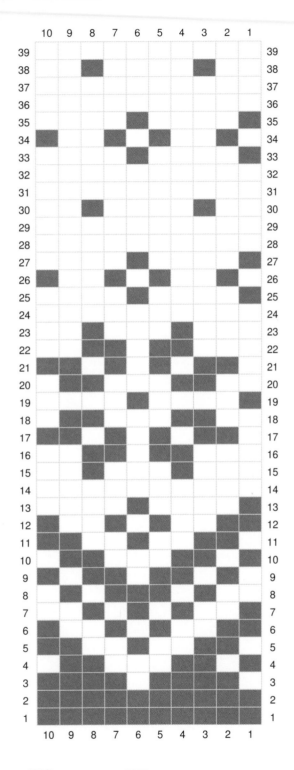

colour A   colour B

LEG

Work the rows of the chart shown opposite. Note that the chart repeats 4, 5, 5 (6, 6) 7, 8, 9 [10] times per round.

Rep rnds 24–39 until work measures 8.25, 8.25, 8.25 (11.5, 11.5) 14, 14, 14, [14]cm/3¼, 3¼, 3¼ (4½, 4½) 5½, 5½, 5½ [5½]in from co edge. Note: When you reach the desired length, ensure you end on a plain rnd with colour A (i.e rnds 28, 31, 36 or 39).

HEEL OPENING – AFTERTHOUGHT HEEL SET UP

Using scrap yarn, k the first 20, 25, 25 (30, 30) 35, 40, 45 [50] sts, then sl scrap yarn sts back onto LH needle.

FOOT

Work rnds 1–39 once and then rep rnds 24–39 until work measures 5, 5.75, 8.25 (9, 10.75) 14, 16, 17.74 [19]cm/2, 2¼, 3¼ (3½, 4¼) 5½, 6¼, 7 [7½]in from heel opening or 7, 8.25, 9.5 (10.25, 10.25) 12, 12, 14 [14]cm/2¾, 3¼, 3¾ (4, 4) 4¾, 4¾, 5½ [5½]in shorter than desired foot length. Note: When you reach the desired length, ensure you end on a plain rnd with colour A (i.e rnds 28, 31, 36, 39).

TOE SHAPING

The toe is worked in the rnd in colour B. Count half your sts and place additional marker.
Rnd 1: *ssk, k to 2 sts before marker, k2tog* rep to end of rnd (4 dec).
Rnd 2: k to end of rnd.
Rep rnds 1 and 2 a total of 5, 6, 6 (7, 7) 8, 8, 8 [8] times. You have 20, 26, 26 (32, 32) 38, 48, 58 [68] sts.
Rep rnd 1 a total of 3, 4, 4 (5, 5) 6, 8, 9 [9] times. You have 8, 10, 10 (12, 12) 14, 16, 22 [32] sts.
Cut yarn, leaving a 30cm/12in tail. Graft rem sts together using kitchener stitch.

AFTERTHOUGHT HEEL

The heel is worked in the rnd using colour B.
Remove scrap yarn to prepare for knitting the heel. Place 20, 25, 25 (30, 30) 35, 40, 45 [50] leg sts on one needle, pick up 1 st at each end. Place 20, 25, 25 (30, 30) 35, 40, 45 [50] foot sts on one needle, pick up 1 st at each end. You have 22, 27, 27 (32, 32) 37, 42, 47 [52] sts on each needle for a total of 44, 54, 54 (64, 64) 74, 84, 94 [104] sts.

SET-UP RND

Pm at beginning of first needle to mark bor. Attach colour B, leaving a tail of at least 15cm/6in.

Rnd 1: K 22, 27, 27 (32, 32) 37, 42, 47 [52] sts, pm, k to end of rnd. Note: If desired, twist picked up "corner" sts to eliminate holes.

Rnd 2: K to end of rnd.

HEEL DECS

Rnd 1: *Ssk, k to 2 sts before marker, k2tog* rep to end of rnd (4 dec).

Rnd 2: K to end of rnd.

Rep rnds 1 and 2 a total of 6, 7, 7 (8, 8) 10, 11, 12 [12] times. You have 20, 26, 26 (32, 32) 34, 40, 46 [56] sts.

Rep rnd 1 a total of 2, 3, 3 (4, 4) 4, 5, 6 [8] times. You have 12, 14, 14 (16, 16) 18, 20, 22 [24] sts.

Cut yarn, leaving a tail of 30cm/12in. Graft rem sts together using kitchener stitch.

SECOND SOCK

If you want to knit a matching pair, rep the above steps for your second sock. To knit a mismatched pair as shown here, reverse the colours, knitting colour A as colour B and vice versa.

FINISHING

Weave in all ends. Wet block socks to measurements.

"IN MY LITTLE CORNER OF THE WORLD WHERE WINTER LINGERS FOR MORE THAN HALF THE YEAR, I FIND COMFORT IN MAKING MY OWN WOOLLY GARMENTS."

WILLOW MITTENS

The motifs on this design is from the delicate yet resilient Arctic willow plant. In summer, Arctic willow germinates puffy seed pods that act as little greenhouses to insulate themselves.

NOTES

The colourwork chart is read from bottom to top and right to left. These mittens are designed as a mismatched pair, as shown here, with colours A and B reversed. For the second mitten, you simply knit colour A as colour B and vice versa. If you prefer, you can modify the pattern to knit two identical mittens by simply not reversing the colours as instructed in the pattern for mitten two. Please swatch to ensure you have the right gauge before beginning. Stranded colourwork might affect your usual gauge so remember to adjust the needle size as needed.

CONSTRUCTION

These mitts are knitted from bottom-up and in the round. The pair features a colourwork motif throughout. The thumb is a gussetless thumb and uses the afterthought thumb technique. The final mitten top stitches are grafted together using kitchener stitch.

SIZES

S (M) L

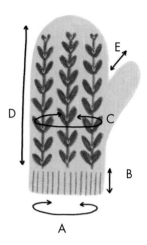

MEASUREMENTS
A: CUFF CIRCUMFERENCE
cm: 16.5 (18) 19
in: 6½ (7) 7½

B: CUFF LENGTH
cm: 4 (5) 5
in: 1½ (2) 2

C: HAND CIRCUMFERENCE
cm: 18 (19) 20
in: 7 (7½) 8

D: HAND LENGTH
cm: 15 (16.5) 18
in: 6 (6½) 7

E: THUMB LENGTH
cm: 3 (4) 4.5
in: 1¼ (1½) 1¾

YARN
Sonder Yarn Co. Sunday Morning (75% Bluefaced Leicester, 25% Masham, DK (light worsted) weight)
Colour A – Offline
Colour B – Dirty weekend

YARDAGE
Calculated based on mismatched pair

COLOUR A
Metres: 50 (65) 80
Yards: 55 (71) 88

COLOUR B
Metres: 50 (65) 80
Yards: 55 (71) 88

GAUGE
24 sts x 26 rnds = 10cm/4in in colourwork sts

NEEDLES
3.25mm/US3 and 3.5mm/US4 needles or sizes necessary to obtain gauge. Use either DPNs, two 60cm/24in circular needles or one longer circular needle for the magic loop method.

NOTIONS
Stitch markers
Scrap yarn
Tapestry needle

BEGIN PATTERN – LEFT MITT/CUFF

Using your choice of stretchy co method, the smaller needles and colour A, co 48 (54) 66 sts. If working with DPNs, divide sts equally across needles. If using the magic loop technique or two circular needles, place half the sts on each needle. Join in the rnd, taking care not to twist sts. Pm to mark bor. Work *k1, p1* ribbing until cuff measures 4 (5) 5cm 1½ (2) 2in from co edge.

HAND

Switch to larger needles. Work the rows of the chart shown below. Note that the chart repeats 8 (9) 10 times per round. Rep rnds 1–8 until work measures 7 (8) 9cm/ ¾ (3¼) 3½in from co edge.

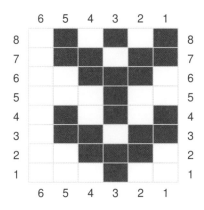

colour A   colour B

THUMB HOLE

With colour A, k1. Using scrap yarn, k the next 7 (8) 9 sts, then sl scrap yarn sts back onto LH needle.

HAND – CONT'D

Work across the scrap yarn sts following the chart, then cont working the rows of the chart until work is 1cm/¼in shorter than the tip of your middle finger.

MITT DECS

Mitt decreases are worked in colour A. Count half the stitches and place a unique marker.
Dec rnd: *K1, ssk, k to 3 sts before marker, k2tog, k1* to end of rnd (4 sts dec).
Rep dec rnd a total of 7 (8) 10 times. You have 20 (22) 26 sts. Cut yarn, leaving a 30cm/12in tail. Graft rem sts together using kitchener stitch.

AFTERTHOUGHT THUMB

The thumb is worked in the rnd using colour A. Remove scrap yarn to prepare for knitting the thumb. Place 7 (8) 9 sts on one needle, pick up 1 st at each end. Place the next 7 (8) 9 sts on next needle, pick up 1 sts at each end. You have 18 (20) 22 sts.
Knit all sts until thumb is approx 1cm/¼in shorter than the tip of your thumb. Work *k2tog* until 5 (5) 6 sts remain. Cut yarn, leaving a 30cm/12in tail. Thread a tapestry needle with the tail and draw it through all sts on needles. Pull up tightly and secure.

RIGHT MITT

If you want to knit a matching pair, rep all the above steps for your right mitt. To knit a mismatched pair as shown here, knit all the colour A sts with colour B and vice versa.

RIGHT MITT THUMB HOLE

With colour B, k 17 (19) 24 sts. Using scrap yarn, k the next 7 (8) 9 sts, sl scrap yarn sts back to LH needle. Cont hand section using instructions above.

FINISHING

Weave in all ends. Wet block to measurements.

"KNITTING IS SLOW, ARGUABLY THE SLOWEST OF SLOW FASHION. EVERY STITCH IN THE ART OF KNITTING IS INTENTIONAL – FROM DESIGNING AND SWATCHING TO ACTUAL KNITTING, EVERY STEP IN THE PROCESS IS A CONSCIOUS CHOICE."

SUPPLIERS

The yarn used to create the designs in this book were generously sponsored by the following yarn dyers and producers. These are yarn companies whose values align with mine in terms of sustainability and ethicality. You can find the exact yarn on their websites by following the link below.

- Anatolia and Nurtured Fine by Julie Asselin (julie-asselin.com)
- Classic by Cardiff Cashmere (cardiffcashmere.it)
- Manchelopi by WoolDreamers and Mont Tricot (wooldreamers.com)
- Mota by WoolDreamers and Mont Tricot (monttricot.getpayd.com)
- Le Petit Lambswool by Biches et Bûches (bichesetbuches.com)
- Lettlopi by Istex (istex.is)
- Shetland/Romney 4ply by Woollen Twine (woollentwine.com)
- Stone Soup DK by Bare Naked Wools (barenakedwools.com)
- Sunday Morning DK by Sonder Yarn Co (sonderyarnco.com)
- Trusty Sock Base by Big Little Yarn Co (biglittleyarn.com)

ACKNOWLEDGEMENTS

This book was the better half of the past year of my life, and never did it cross my mind that I would get to this point. To my biggest supporter who gave me life, who gave me the space to grow into who I am today, who never limited my dreams, who never forced me down a career path, who never insisted I fit into the mould, to my dad, thank you. I wouldn't be half the person I am without your unconditional love, sacrifice and acceptance. Thank you for trusting me to make my own decisions, to go on the wildest adventures and to explore and venture into this world.

Thank you, Theo – I am forever grateful our paths crossed. I am so, so, so glad we met and shared a huge part of our lives together. Thank you for putting me first all those years. Thank you for being supportive of all the rabbit holes I burrow into. One of those tunnels I went down led me here, and I am thankful for you being part of this journey. To Alex, who I met on my second day in Oslo – our short five months together made us lifelong friends, I can't say thank you enough. I am happy we adopted each other from the very first day and I am even happier we have chosen to be in each other's lives despite a huge pond separating us. Without you, I would never have learned to knit. Thank you for being the person who made me thepetiteknitter. I can't wait to meet baby Llopis-Metenier!

Win Shi, thank you for being a constant in my life. Thank you for the past 13 years of friendship, for listening to all my unfiltered thoughts, for knowing me, for supporting me, for always being there for me. Thank you for being my rock. To everyone else who made this book a reality, thank you. To Grant, who took the time to drive us out on the land, who made sure the cabin was warm and toasty every time I got in. To Casey, who listened to my hours of rants and uncertainties.

Thank you to Harriet at Quadrille for reaching out to me two years ago, who decided my work was worthy of a book. Thank you to Kim, my ever-patient photographer who travelled two days to get to the Arctic, who was up for photographing in any conditions and any time of the day, who was smiling even when I was tired, cranky, and cold. Thank you to Gemma, the fantastic designer of this book. Thank you to my sample knitters, Heidi, Fiona, Teresa, Francois, and Claudio. Thank you to all of you who have supported thepetiteknitter over the years. This book would not have been here without any of you.

ABOUT THE AUTHOR

Weichien Chan is the author of ARCTIC KNITS. She is the person behind @thepetiteknitter. She is a knitter, a designer, an INTP and an avid traveller.

MANAGING DIRECTOR Sarah Lavelle
SENIOR COMMISSIONING EDITOR Harriet Butt
COPYEDITOR Salima Hirani
SENIOR DESIGNER Gemma Hayden
ASSISTANT DESIGNER Alicia House
PHOTOGRAPHER Kim Lightbody
MODELS Freyja (cat), Saskie (bunny), Theo Potgieter,
  and Weichien Chan
HEAD OF PRODUCTION Stephen Lang
SENIOR PRODUCTION CONTROLLER Gary Hayes

Published in 2023 by Quadrille,
an imprint of Hardie Grant Publishing

Quadrille
52–54 Southwark Street
London SE1 1UN
quadrille.com

Cataloguing in Publication Data: a catalogue record for
this book is available from the British Library

Text and knitwear designs © Weichien Chan 2024
Photography © Kim Lightbody 2024
Design and layout © Quadrille 2024

ISBN 978 1 787 139 985

Printed in China using soy inks